gettyimages

1900s

Decades of the 20th Century
Décadas del siglo XX
Decadi del XX secolo

Decades of the 20th Century
Décadas del siglo XX
Decadi del XX secolo

Nick Yapp

KÖNEMANN

This book was produced by Getty Images
Unique House, 21–31 Woodfield Road, London W9 2BA

For KÖNEMANN:	For Getty Images:
Managing editor: Sally Bald	Art director: Michael Rand
Project editors: Lucile Bas, Meike Hilbring	Design: B+B
	Picture editor: Ali Khoja
	Editor: Richard Collins
	Proof reader: Elisabeth Ihre
	Editorial assistance: Tom Worsley
	Special thanks: Tea McAleer

© 2004 for the trilingual edition in English, Spanish and Italian:
Tandem Verlag GmbH
KÖNEMANN is a trademark and an imprint of Tandem Verlag GmbH
Spanish translation: Josep Mª Jovells i Salvia for LocTeam, S. L., Barcelona
Italian translation: Quirino Di Zitti for LocTeam, S. L., Barcelona
Text editing and typesetting: LocTeam, S. L., Barcelona

Printed in China

ISBN 3-8331-1145-3

10 9 8 7 6 5 4 3
X IX VIII VII VI V IV III II I

Frontispiece: The sun shines on Edwardian society. The proud and the fashionable
arrive at Henley railway station for the annual regatta, 4 June 1905. The London
Season was at its height – ahead lay weeks of washing and ironing for the domestics.

Frontispicio: Luce un magnífico sol en la sociedad de Eduardo VII. Las elites y las
clases altas llegan a la estación de Henley para asistir a la regata anual, el 4 de junio
de 1905. La temporada londinense está llegando a su punto álgido, y a los empleados
del servicio doméstico les quedan todavía algunas semanas de duro trabajo.

Frontespizio: Splende il sole sul regno di Edoardo VII. 4 giugno 1905, il fior fiore
della società giunge alla stazione di Henley per l'annuale regata. La stagione londinese
è al suo apogeo… e i domestici avranno montagne di panni da lavare e stirare per
intere settimane.

Contents / Contenido / Sommario

Introduction 6
Introducción 8
Introduzione 10

1. Cabbages and kings
   Esplendor y miseria
   Cavoli e re 12

2. Conflict
   Conflictos
   Conflitti 36

3. Peoples
   Gentes
   Popoli 64

4. Migration
   Migraciones
   Migrazioni 84

5. Haves and have-nots
   Ricos y pobres
   Ricchi e poveri 102

6. Work
   Trabajo
   Lavoro 124

7. Leisure
   Ocio
   Tempo libero 164

8. Entertainment
   Espectáculos
   Spettacolo 194

9. The Arts
   Las artes
   Arte 220

10. Fashion
    Moda
    Moda 246

11. Science
    Ciencia
    Scienza 268

12. Transport
    Transporte
    Mezzi di trasporto 292

13. Sport
    Deporte
    Sport 316

14. Children
    Los más pequeños
    Bambini 346

15. All human life
    Cosas de la vida
    Fatti della vita 370

    Index 399

Introduction

The last sprint to the finishing line of the 19th century produced a host of inventions and innovations to launch the 20th century on its mad and merry way. There was the telephone, the telegraph, the automobile, cinematography, the X-ray, the discovery of radioactivity, the gramophone, synthetic fibres, the cathode ray, the steam turbine and a thousand other wonders, all products of the 1890s. The vocabulary, as well as the quality, of life changed almost beyond measure.

The great work on hand was rivalry – commercial, military, technical and scientific. The great powers of Europe were the most concerned. Their rivalry encompassed the globe. France, Germany and Britain measured each other's industrial might and devoted vast resources to catching up with the others or maintaining their lead. Imperial Russia watched with concern, but had trouble enough controlling its own population. The United States begged to be left alone, while seizing the chance to tighten its grip on Central America.

Away from the laboratory or the parade ground, the shipyard or the factory bench, the move to frivolity continued. Crowds flocked to music-halls, cabarets, vaudeville theatres, dance floors, movie parlours and cafés. A glass of wine or beer and a cheap cigar gave Everyman a chance to feel like a Rockefeller. Women took up smoking and drinking in public, and every kind of sport. They learnt how to drive a car and how not to have babies – though the former skill was more easily attained.

The rich dashed from one exciting event to another – the opera, the races, regattas, balls, shoots, foxhunts, presentations at Court – for the royal trade union still had many paid-up members. The poor staggered from slum to sweatshop and back again, though their own trade unions were slowly winning the struggle for better wages, shorter working hours, and safety at work. All over the world suffragettes fought for the right to vote. In a few places they were successful. Immigrants to the United States continued to pour into Ellis Island, seeking new life, new liberty, new hope. In a few cases they were successful.

And so into the brand new century. Subways were opened in New York and Paris. There was a new oil company called Standard Oil, a new disposable razor marketed by Mr Gillette, a new power source called a 'battery' made by Thomas Edison, a new automobile manufacturing company owned by Henry Ford. It was the decade of the first World Series (baseball), the first Tour de France (cycling) and the first Nobel prizes; of art nouveau and the Brownie camera; of the *Potemkin* mutiny and the San Francisco earthquake; of Pavlov's dogs and Charles Dana Gibson's 'Girls'.

The Wright brothers flew a heavier-than-air machine across the sands of Kitty Hawk, North Carolina, and Louis Blériot piloted the first plane to cross the Channel. Britain, it was said, was no longer an island. Did it matter? There was a new alliance between France and Britain – the Entente Cordiale – a pledge of help and friendship between two hitherto perennial foes. Better means of communication promised greater understanding between nations. But, as the next decade was to prove, old grudges ran deep…

Introducción

El último *sprint* hasta cruzar la meta del siglo XIX fue testigo de numerosos inventos y descubrimientos que prepararon el camino a un siglo de locuras pero también de bienestar: el siglo XX. El teléfono, el telégrafo, el automóvil, el cine, los rayos X, el descubrimiento de la radioactividad, el gramófono, las fibras sintéticas, los rayos catódicos, las turbinas de vapor y mil maravillas más vieron la luz durante la década de 1890. El vocabulario, además de la calidad de vida, cambió de una forma extraordinaria.

En el nuevo escenario, el concepto clave es la rivalidad, tanto comercial como militar, técnica o científica, y los actores principales son las grandes potencias europeas. Todo el planeta estaba inmerso en una vorágine de rivalidad. Francia, Alemania y Gran Bretaña competían en poder industrial y dedicaban ingentes recursos a mantener su liderazgo o superar a los demás países. La Rusia imperial contemplaba el panorama con cierta preocupación, pero estaba muy ocupada en controlar a su propio pueblo, y Estados Unidos prefería un papel secundario mientras esperaba la oportunidad de extender su poder por América Central.

Lejos del laboratorio o los cuarteles militares, de los astilleros o las fábricas, la vida comenzaba a teñirse de una cierta frivolidad. La gente acudía en masa a los *music-halls*, cabarés, salas de baile, cines y cafés. Con un vaso de vino en la mano y un puro barato entre los labios, cualquiera podía sentirse Rockefeller por un instante. Las mujeres comenzaron a fumar y beber en público y a practicar deportes reservados hasta entonces a los hombres. También aprendieron a conducir y a controlar su fertilidad, aunque quizá dominaron antes lo primero que lo segundo.

Los ricos iban y venían de un acontecimiento a otro: ópera, carreras, regatas, bailes, cacerías, pleitos, etc. No en vano, el Sindicato de Comercio Real contaba aún con muchos miembros "asalariados". En cambio, los pobres vivían sumidos en la miseria de los barrios bajos y la explotación laboral –si bien los sindicatos obreros empezaban a ganar la batalla para conseguir sueldos dignos, jornadas más cortas y seguridad en el trabajo–. En todo el mundo empezaba a ganar terreno el movimiento que luchaba por el voto femenino, pero solo se logró en algunos países. Los inmigrantes que llegaban a Estados Unidos seguían pasando por Ellis Island en busca de una nueva vida, libertad y esperanza. También solo algunos lo consiguieron.

Así comenzó el nuevo siglo. Se inauguraron los metros de Nueva York y París. Surgió una nueva empresa petrolera, la Standard Oil; apareció en el mercado una nueva navaja de afeitar desechable, inventada por K. C. Gillete; Thomas Edison creó una nueva fuente de energía, la batería, y Henry Ford abrió una fábrica de automóviles. Durante la primera década del siglo XX se celebraron la primera World Series (campeonato mundial de béisbol) y el primer Tour de Francia (ciclismo), y se concedió el primer premio Nobel. Fue la época del modernismo, de la rebelión del acorazado *Potemkin* y del terremoto de San Francisco, y también de los perros de Pavlov y de las "chicas Gibson".

Los hermanos Wright hicieron volar un artefacto más pesado que el aire sobre la región de Kitty Hawk, en Carolina del Norte, y Louis Blériot cruzó por primera vez el canal de la Mancha en avión. Tal como solía decirse, Gran Bretaña ya no era una isla. Pero no importaba. Existía una nueva alianza entre Francia y Gran Bretaña, la Entente Cordiale, un compromiso de ayuda y amistad entre dos antiguos enemigos. La mejora en los medios de comunicación prometía una mayor comprensión entre los países, pero el tiempo se encargaría de demostrar que los rencores del pasado aún no habían desaparecido…

Introduzione

Lo sprint finale verso la linea d'arrivo del XIX secolo porta con sé una miriade di invenzioni e di innovazioni che apriranno il nuovo secolo con gioia ed entusiasmo. Il telefono, il telegrafo, l'automobile, il cinematografo, i raggi X, la scoperta della radioattività, il grammofono, le fibre sintetiche, i raggi catodici, la turbina a vapore e altre innumerevoli meraviglie sono tutti prodotti di questo decennio. Cambia radicalmente il vocabolario, assieme alla qualità della vita quotidiana.

La parola d'ordine è concorrenza: commerciale, militare, tecnica e scientifica, soprattutto tra le grandi potenze europee, che coinvolgono il mondo intero nella loro rivalità. La Francia, la Germania e la Gran Bretagna mettono a confronto la loro potenza nel settore industriale dedicando grandi risorse per tenere il passo delle altre nazioni o per mantenere la loro supremazia. La Russia imperiale osserva con preoccupazione, impegnata anche troppo nel controllare il suo popolo. Gli Stati Uniti preferiscono restare in disparte, e colgono l'occasione per stringere la loro morsa sull'America Centrale.

Lontano dai laboratori, dalle piazze d'armi, dai cantieri navali e dalle fabbriche, la gente continua ad apprezzare le frivolezze della vita, e accorre in massa a music-hall, cabaret, varietà, sale da ballo, cinematografi e caffè. Con un bicchier di vino o di birra ed un sigaro da pochi soldi, chiunque ha la possibilità di sentirsi come un Rockefeller. Le donne fumano e bevono in pubblico e praticano ogni tipo di sport. Hanno imparato a guidare la macchina e ad evitare di avere figli – anche se è ancora più facile guidare che accedere ai metodi contraccettivi.

I più facoltosi corrono da un'emozione all'altra – opera, corse di cavalli, regate, balli, gare di tiro, cacce alla volpe, presentazioni a corte – dato che le monarchie hanno ancora molti seguaci. I più poveri si trascinano dalle loro catapecchie alle fabbriche schiaviste, anche se i sindacati iniziano a vincere le prime battaglie per uno stipendio migliore, un orario più corto e una maggiore sicurezza sul lavoro. In tutto il mondo, le suffragiste lottano per il diritto al voto e in alcuni luoghi lo conquistano. Negli Stati Uniti, gli immigranti continuano a riversarsi a Ellis Island, lottando per una nuova vita, per la libertà, per una speranza, e in alcuni casi le conquistano.

Si entra così nel nuovo secolo. New York e Parigi inaugurano le rispettive metropolitane. Nasce una nuova compagnia petrolifera, la Standard Oil, un nuovo rasoio usa e getta, brevettato da un certo Gillette, una nuova fonte di energia chiamata "batteria", ideata da Thomas Edison, una nuova fabbrica di automobili, quella di Henry Ford. È il decennio della prima World Series di baseball, del primo Tour de France e dei primi premi Nobel; dell'art nouveau e della cinepresa Brownie; dell'ammutinamento sulla corazzata *Potemkin* e del terremoto di San Francisco; dei cani di Pavlov e delle "Gibson Girl" di Charles Dana Gibson.

I fratelli Wright spiccano il volo con un apparecchio più pesante dell'aria sulla spiaggia di Kitty Hawk, nella Carolina del Nord, mentre Louis Blériot sorvola per primo il canale della Manica. La Gran Bretagna, si dice allora, non è più un'isola. Ma cosa importa? La Gran Bretagna e la Francia firmano una nuova alleanza – l'Entente Cordiale – una promessa di aiuto e di amicizia tra le due eterne antagoniste. I mezzi di comunicazione fanno passi da gigante, annunciando una maggiore intesa tra le varie nazioni. Ma il decennio successivo dimostrerà che le vecchie ferite non sono ancora cicatrizzate…

1. Cabbages and kings
Esplendor y miseria
Cavoli e re

The Old Lady of Windsor is finally laid to rest. Crowds line the route of Queen Victoria's funeral cortège as it passes through London in the winter of 1901. For Britain an era had ended, and the 20th century was truly about to begin.

La vieja Dama de Windsor descansa en paz para siempre. Las multitudes inundan las calles de Londres al paso del cortejo fúnebre de la reina Victoria, en el invierno de 1901. Terminaba una era para Gran Bretaña y el siglo XX estaba a punto de comenzar de verdad.

La vecchia Lady di Windsor è accompagnata al riposo eterno. A Londra, nell'inverno del 1901, la gente si affolla lungo il percorso del corteo funebre della regina Vittoria. Per la Gran Bretagna si chiude un'epoca, il XX secolo è già alle porte.

1. Cabbages and kings
Esplendor y miseria
Cavoli e re

It was the final fling for unashamed splendour – a time when monarchs dressed themselves in all their Ruritanian glory, though it did little for their personal protection. For all their pomp and majesty, few kings slept easily at night.

The extravagantly rich dwelt in marble halls on which they frittered away only a few of the millions that they had made from railways, banking, iron and steel, oil and shipping. The unfortunate masses on the whole respected the lucky few, though organised labour fought more vociferously for better working conditions and shorter hours.

There were signs of change. Democracy was on the advance; socialism was on the march. Norway and Bulgaria gained their independence, while Bosnia and Herzegovina fell under the control of Austria – a change that was to bring misery to millions a decade later. For the first time, the right of the white man to do whatever he wanted was challenged in India and Africa.

Visually, it was a beautiful age. Socially, it was disgraceful. Politically, it was exciting and alarming. But there were always the charms of the Palm Court and the Winter Gardens, and life – for some – was sweeter than it had ever been.

Tocaba a su fin una época de esplendor sin reparos, un tiempo en que los monarcas vestían como si fueran pequeños dioses, aunque ello no les daba más seguridad. A pesar de tanta pompa y majestuosidad, pocos reyes dormían realmente tranquilos por la noche.

Los más excesivos entre los ricos vivían en casas con vestíbulos de mármol, donde derrochaban solo algunos de los muchos millones que habían ganado gracias al ferrocarril, la banca, la industria del hierro y el acero, el petróleo y la navegación. Generalmente, las masas aceptaban su suerte y respetaban a los ricos, pero cada vez se organizaban de manera más eficaz para obtener mejores condiciones de trabajo y jornadas más cortas.

Los tiempos estaban cambiando. La democracia se iba extendiendo y el socialismo progresaba. Noruega y Bulgaria alcanzaron la independencia, mientras que Bosnia y Herzegovina cayeron bajo el dominio de Austria, un hecho que traería la miseria a millones de personas en la década siguiente. Por primera vez en la historia, en India y en África se puso en duda el supuesto derecho del hombre blanco a dominar el mundo.

Desde un punto de vista estético, fue una época bella, pero en los aspectos sociales dejó mucho que desear. En política se vivieron unos años emocionantes, pero también alarmantes. De todas formas, siempre quedaban los encantos de Palm Court y Winter Gardens. Durante aquellos años, la vida enseñó su cara más amable, al menos para algunos.

Sono gli ultimi anni in cui la monarchia mostra spudoratamente la sua magnificenza, ostentando abiti da fiaba di poca utilità per la difesa della propria persona. Malgrado i fasti e la maestosità, nessuno di loro dorme sonni tranquilli.

I più facoltosi sperperano, nei loro saloni di marmo, una minima parte delle immense ricchezze accumulate con le ferrovie, le banche, il ferro e l'acciaio, il petrolio ed il commercio. Le classi meno agiate rispettano, in generale, questi pochi fortunati, anche se le organizzazioni sindacali reclamano a gran voce migliori condizioni e meno ore di lavoro.

I tempi stanno per cambiare. La democrazia avanza a scapito del socialismo. La Norvegia e la Bulgaria conquistano l'indipendenza, mentre la Bosnia e l'Erzegovina cadono sotto il controllo dell'Austria – evento che si rivelerà funesto per milioni di persone un decennio più tardi. Per la prima volta, in India e in Africa l'uomo bianco vede minacciato il suo diritto di fare ciò che vuole.

Un'epoca meravigliosa per gli occhi ma tragica per la società, anni di grandi emozioni e preoccupazioni per i governanti. Ma il fascino delle corti e dei giardini è ancora intatto, e la vita – per alcuni – scivola via più dolce che mai.

On to centre stage steps a new monarch:
Edward VII poses for his likeness, c. 1901.
He was 60 years old when he succeeded
to the throne.

Entra en escena un nuevo monarca:
Eduardo VII posa para un retrato, hacia 1901.
Tenía 60 años cuando llegó al trono.

Sale in cattedra un nuovo monarca: Edoardo
VII posa per un ritratto, ca. 1901, anno in
cui, ormai sessantenne, ascende al trono
d'Inghilterra.

A less than flattering view of the new King of England, taken at Sandringham, the royal estate in Norfolk, c. 1901.

Una imagen poco favorecedora del nuevo rey de Inglaterra, tomada en Sandringham, la residencia real de Norfolk, hacia 1901.

Un'immagine poco lusinghiera del nuovo re d'Inghilterra, scattata a Sandringham, la residenza reale nel Norfolk, ca. 1901.

Reinhold Thiele's portrait of Stephanus Johannes Paulus Kruger, leader of the Boers in their fight against Britain. After early successes, the Boers were now heading for defeat.

Retrato de Stephanus Johannes Paulus Kruger, líder de los bóers en lucha contra Gran Bretaña, tomado por Reinhold Thiele. Después de algunos triunfos iniciales, los bóers se encaminaban hacia la derrota final.

Ritratto, eseguito da Reinhold Thiele, di Stephanus Johannes Paulus Kruger, capo dei Boeri durante la guerra contro gli inglesi. Malgrado le vittorie iniziali, i Boeri si avviano verso la sconfitta.

The last Tsar. (Opposite) Kaiser Wilhelm II of Germany extends his hand to his cousin, Tsar Nicholas II of Russia. (Above) Nicholas consults his liver specialist before taking a trip on the royal yacht.

El último zar. (Página anterior) El emperador Guillermo II de Alemania tiende la mano a su primo, el zar Nicolás II de Rusia. (Arriba) El zar Nicolás consulta con su especialista en afecciones hepáticas antes de emprender un viaje en el yate real.

L'ultimo zar. (Pagina a fianco) Il kaiser Guglielmo II di Prussia tende la mano a suo cugino, lo zar Nicola II di Russia. (In alto) Nicola II consulta il suo epatologo prima di intraprendere un viaggio sullo yacht reale.

An upset during a picnic attended by the Russian royal family, c. 1909. There were far worse upsets ahead for Nicholas and his daughter.

Un pequeño contratiempo durante un *picnic* de la familia real rusa, hacia 1909. A Nicolás y su hija les esperaban problemas mucho más graves.

Un piccolo imprevisto durante un picnic con la famiglia reale russa, ca. 1909. Ben altri imprevisti attendono Nicola II e sua figlia.

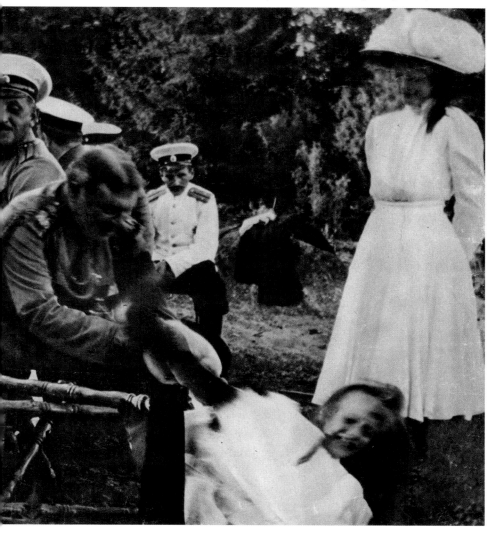

Vladimir Ilyich
Lenin bides his time
and makes his plans
for the revolution
that was to tear
Russia and the
world apart, 1901.

Vladimir Ilich
Lenin aguarda el
momento oportuno
para iniciar la
revolución que
dividiría a Rusia
y al mundo entero,
1901.

Vladimir Ilyich
Lenin, in attesa
del momento
opportuno, prepara
la rivoluzione che
sconvolgerà la
Russia e il mondo
intero, 1901.

President William McKinley of the United States addresses a crowd shortly after his re-election in 1900. McKinley's money-making policies were enormously popular…

El presidente de Estados Unidos, William McKinley, se dirige a una multitud poco después de su reelección en 1900. La política económica de McKinley consiguió superar la crisis y fue enormemente popular…

Il presidente degli Stati Uniti William McKinley si rivolge alla folla subito dopo la rielezione del 1900. La sua politica economica riempie le casse dello stato ed ottiene un enorme successo popolare…

…but not with everyone. A year later, McKinley was shot by an anarchist named Leon Czolgosz at a rally in Buffalo. He died eight days later. McKinley's funeral took place on a rain-drenched day in Washington, DC.

… pero no para todos. Un año más tarde, McKinley fue tiroteado por un anarquista llamado Leon Czolgosz en un mitin en Buffalo. Murió ocho días después. El funeral tuvo lugar en Washington DC en un día lluvioso.

…ma non tutti lo ammirano. Un anno dopo, in un comizio a Buffalo, l'anarchico Leon Czolgosz fa fuoco su McKinley che muore otto giorni più tardi. Il funerale si svolge in una giornata di pioggia a Washington, DC.

On the streets...Winston Spencer Churchill, President of the
Board of Trade, campaigns on the top of a taxi, seeking support
for his new Liberal policies, Manchester, April 1908.

En las calles... Winston Spencer Churchill, presidente de la
Cámara de Comercio, hace campaña desde lo alto de un
taxi para pedir apoyo a su nueva política liberal, Manchester,
abril de 1908.

Giù in strada... Winston Spencer Churchill, ministro del
Commercio, promuove dall'alto di un taxi la sua nuova
politica liberale, Manchester, aprile 1908.

On the stump… Theodore Roosevelt, Governor of New York State, addresses a crowd of suffragettes from the verandah of his home, 1900. 'Votes for Women' was never high on his political agenda.

Haciendo campaña… Theodore Roosevelt, gobernador del estado de Nueva York, se dirige a una multitud de sufragistas desde la galería de su casa, en 1900. El voto de las mujeres nunca figuró entre sus prioridades.

Sulla tribuna… Theodore Roosvelt, governatore dello stato di New York, si rivolge a una folla di suffragette dalla veranda di casa sua, 1900. I voti delle donne non hanno mai avuto troppa importanza per la sua agenda politica.

The white man's game. A young Mohandas Gandhi poses outside his law office in Natal, c. 1903. He had given up a £5,000 a year law practice in Bombay.

El juego del hombre blanco. Un joven Mahatma Gandhi posa en el exterior de su gabinete de abogados en Natal, hacia 1903. Poco antes había abandonado su gabinete de Bombay, que le reportaba 5.000 libras anuales.

Il gioco dell'uomo bianco. Il giovane Mahatma Gandhi posa davanti al suo studio di avvocato nel Natal, ca. 1903. Aveva abbandonato Bombay e la carriera di avvocato che gli rendeva 5.000 sterline l'anno.

The Welshman's game. David Lloyd George and his faithful pug ponder the future, c. 1904. Within the next few years, Lloyd George would do much to challenge the power of inherited wealth.

El juego del galés. David Lloyd George y su fiel doguillo meditan sobre el futuro, hacia 1904. En los años siguientes, Lloyd George desafiaría el poder de las grandes fortunas heredadas.

Il gioco del gallese. David Lloyd George e il suo fedele carlino pensano al futuro, ca. 1904. Negli anni seguenti, Lloyd George sfiderà il potere dei ricchi ereditieri.

Jean Jaurès (third from the left) chats with colleagues on
a French street, c. 1901. Jaurès was the founder of both
the French Socialist Party and the left-wing newspaper
L'Humanité.

Jean Jaurès (tercero por la izquierda) habla con varios colegas
en una calle de Francia, hacia 1901. Jaurès fue el fundador
del Partido Socialista francés y del periódico izquierdista
L'Humanité.

Jean Jaurès (il primo a destra) discute con dei colleghi nelle
strade francesi, ca. 1901. Jaurès è il fondatore del Partito
Socialista Francese e del giornale di sinistra *L'Humanité*.

Ramsay MacDonald – significantly, the only man not wearing a hat, as fashion then decreed – at a Labour Party demonstration in 1909. MacDonald was one of the founders of the British Labour Party.

Ramsay MacDonald, el único hombre que no lleva sombrero, en contra de lo que dictaba la moda de la época, en una manifestación del Partido Laborista, en 1909. MacDonald fue uno de los fundadores del Partido Laborista británico.

Ramsay MacDonald – non a caso l'unico senza cappello, un accessorio obbligatorio per la moda dell'epoca – in una manifestazione del Partito laburista britannico nel 1909. MacDonald fu uno dei fondatori del partito.

Immigrant millionaire. Andrew Carnegie, the Scottish industrialist and philanthropist, at his desk, c. 1900. Carnegie made his fortune in the United States' iron and steel industries.

Un inmigrante millonario. Andrew Carnegie, industrial y filántropo escocés, en su despacho, hacia 1900. Carnegie amasó su fortuna gracias a la industria del hierro y el acero de Estados Unidos.

Un immigrato miliardario. Andrew Carnegie, imprenditore e filantropo scozzese alla sua scrivania, ca. 1900. Carnegie aveva fatto fortuna negli Stati Uniti, nell'industria del ferro e dell'acciaio.

Home-bred millionaire. John Pierpoint Morgan, the American financier, banker and art collector, c. 1909. Morgan founded the US Steel Corporation.

Un millonario del país. John Pierpoint Morgan, hombre de finanzas, banquero y coleccionista de arte americano, hacia 1909. Morgan fundó la US Steel Corporation.

Un miliardario americano. John Pierpoint Morgan, finanziere, banchiere e collezionista d'arte, ca. 1909. Morgan fondò la US Steel Corporation.

2. Conflict
Conflictos
Conflitti

The British Naval Brigade shell Boer positions during the Battle of
Magersfontein in the Second Boer War, December 1900. The gun
was known as 'Joe Chamberlain' after the Secretary for the Colonies.
Hauling it over the rough terrain was a formidable achievement, later
celebrated in the annual field-gun competition at the Royal Tournament.

La Brigada Naval Británica bombardea las posiciones de los bóer durante la
batalla de Magersfontein, durante la segunda guerra Bóer, en diciembre de
1900. El cañón se bautizó con el nombre de "Joe Chamberlain" en honor
al Secretario de las Colonias. Conducirlo por un terreno tan accidentado fue
todo un éxito, que se celebró posteriormente en el concurso anual de
cañones del Torneo Real.

La British Naval Brigade bombarda le posizioni boere nella battaglia di
Magersfontein durante la seconda guerra anglo-boera, dicembre 1900.
Il cannone porta il nome del Segretario per le Colonie Joe Chamberlain. Solo
il fatto di averlo trasportato su un terreno così accidentato rappresentava un
successo formidabile, che verrà poi celebrato nel Torneo Reale annuale dei
cannoni da campagna.

2. Conflict
Conflictos
Conflitti

War was a splendid thing. There were fine new toys to play with – bigger guns than ever before, torpedoes, great battleships, submarines, and even early chemical weapons. Few thought that the fledgling aeroplane would be of any use, but there was still the cavalry to add tone to what would otherwise have been a mere vulgar brawl.

And there were plenty of places in which these new weapons could be tried out. The British army was active in South Africa from 1899 to 1902, in Tibet in 1903 and in India throughout the entire decade. Germany and France kept a watchful and suspicious eye on the annual manoeuvres of each other's armies and navies. Russia marched proudly into Manchuria in 1900 and suffered an ignominious defeat at the hands of the Japanese in 1905.

Civil disturbances abounded. There were riots in Madrid in 1900, and a near-revolution in Barcelona nine years later. The Boxer Rebellion against foreign interference in Chinese affairs was crushed with savage cruelty.

And, though few realised it at the time, when the Young Bosnia movement began terrorist activities against the Austro-Hungarian Empire, the time to open the boxes of the new toys of destruction came considerably nearer.

Para algunos, la guerra tenía la emoción de un juego, y, ciertamente, con el nuevo siglo llegaron nuevos "juguetes": cañones de gran calibre, torpedos, enormes buques de guerra, submarinos, e incluso las primeras armas químicas. Pocos imaginaron entonces que aquellos primitivos aeroplanos pudieran tener alguna aplicación militar, y la caballería aún era la estrella en cualquier conflicto.

Por desgracia, había muchos lugares donde ensayar con las nuevas armas. El ejército británico actuó en Sudáfrica entre 1899 y 1902, en el Tíbet en 1903 y en la India a lo largo de toda la década. Alemania y Francia se vigilaban de cerca mutuamente, controlando las maniobras que realizaban cada año sus respectivos ejércitos y flotas. Rusia ocupó Manchuria en 1900, pero sufrió una estrepitosa derrota contra los japoneses en 1905.

En todas partes había disturbios. En 1900 hubo revueltas callejeras en Madrid, y nueve años más tarde estuvo a punto de estallar una revolución en Barcelona. La Rebelión bóxer contra la injerencia extranjera en China fue aplastada de forma brutal.

Aunque entonces pocos se dieron cuenta de ello, cuando el movimiento para la Joven Bosnia inició sus actividades terroristas contra el imperio austrohúngaro, faltaba poco para que se abriera definitivamente la caja de Pandora de los nuevos juguetes de destrucción.

Dicevano che la guerra era una cosa meravigliosa. Nascevano dei nuovissimi giocattoli – enormi cannoni mai visti prima, siluri, grandi corazzate, sommergibili e perfino le prime armi chimiche. Erano in pochi a pensare che i novelli aeroplani potessero servire a qualcosa, ma c'era ancora la cavalleria a mantenere alto il livello di quelle che, altrimenti, sarebbero state considerate alla stregua di volgari risse.

E c'erano tantissimi luoghi in cui provare le nuove armi. L'esercito britannico opera in Sud Africa dal 1899 al 1902, in Tibet nel 1903 ed in India per l'intero decennio. La Germania e la Francia osservano con sospetto le manovre annuali dei rispettivi eserciti. Nel 1900, la Russia marcia con arroganza sulla Manciuria e soffre una umiliante sconfitta da parte dei giapponesi nel 1905.

Le rivolte civili scoppiano dappertutto: a Madrid nel 1900 e a Barcellona, quasi una rivoluzione, nove anni più tardi. La Rivolta dei Boxer contro l'interferenza straniera in Cina viene schiacciata con crudeltà selvaggia.

E, anche se all'epoca nessuno se ne rese conto, quando il movimento irredentista Giovane Bosnia iniziò le sue azioni terroriste contro l'Impero austroungarico, era ormai giunto il momento di tirare fuori i nuovi giocattoli di distruzione.

A group of British prisoners of war in the early days of the Boer War (1899–1902). On the right is Winston Churchill, twenty-five-year-old war correspondent of the *Morning Post*. He escaped and hurried back to England, where he became an MP.

Un grupo de prisioneros de guerra británicos al principio de la guerra Bóer (1899–1902). A la derecha aparece Winston Churchill, a sus 25 años, corresponsal de guerra del *Morning Post*, que consiguió escapar y regresar a Inglaterra, donde se convirtió en diputado parlamentario.

Un gruppo di prigionieri di guerra britannici nei primi giorni della Guerra anglo-boera (1899–1902). Sulla destra, il venticinquenne Winston Churchill, corrispondente di guerra del *Morning Post*, tornerà in fretta e furia in Inghilterra per poi assumere la carica di deputato.

Armed Afrikaaners (Boers) pose for the camera during the siege of Ladysmith, 1900. The Boers were well-armed, superbly mounted and experts in *veldt* craft, but their early victories gave way to a series of bitter defeats.

Afrikáners armados (bóers) posan para la cámara durante el sitio de Ladysmith, en 1900. Los bóers estaban bien armados, eran excelentes jinetes y conocían bien el *veldt* (la estepa sudafricana), pero sus victorias iniciales dieron paso a una serie de amargas derrotas.

Afrikaner (boeri) armati posano durante l'assedio di Ladysmith, nel 1900. I boeri erano bene armati, eccellenti cavalieri ed esperti del veldt (steppa dell'Africa del Sud), ma i successi iniziali furono presto cancellati da una serie di amare sconfitte.

British dead in front of a Boer defence post. Losses on both sides were
heavy during the Boer War. The British were unused to a war of movement,
and to the guerrilla tactics of the Boers. They were also incompetently led.

Víctimas británicas ante un puesto de defensa bóer. Durante la guerra Bóer
se produjeron numerosas bajas en ambos bandos. Los británicos no estaban
acostumbrados a una guerra con tanta movilidad ni a las tácticas guerrilleras
de los bóer, y además sus mandos militares se revelaron incompetentes.

Caduti britannici davanti a un avamposto di difesa boero. Nella Guerra
anglo-boera, entrambe le parti subirono gravi perdite. Gli inglesi non erano
abituati alle guerre di movimento e alle tattiche di guerriglia dei boeri. E come
se non bastasse, erano guidati da ufficiali incompetenti.

Reinhold Thiele's study of Boer dead on the battlefield of Spion Kop, 24 January 1900. It had been typical battle of the war, a desperate struggle for possession of high ground that was ultimately of little use to either side.

Estudio de Reinhold Thiele sobre las víctimas bóer en el campo de batalla de Spion Kop, 24 de enero de 1900. Fue una de las típicas batallas de esta guerra, una lucha desesperada por el control de una meseta que finalmente sirvió de poco para ambos bandos.

Una fotografia di Reinhold Thiele: caduti boeri a Spion Kop, 24 gennaio 1900. Una battaglia tipica di questa guerra, una lotta disperata per conquistare una collina che, in fin dei conti, era di ben poca utilità per entrambi gli eserciti.

Another of Reinhold Thiele's grimly
beautiful images from the Boer War.
A blindfolded German intermediary is
brought in from the Boer lines to negotiate
a surrender, 17 March 1900.

Otra de las bellas y polvorientas imágenes
de Reinhold Thiele tomada durante la
guerra Bóer. Un mediador alemán con los
ojos vendados abandona unos instantes las
líneas bóers para negociar una rendición,
17 de marzo de 1900.

Ancora un'immagine sinistra e affascinante
di Reinhold Thiele dalla Guerra anglo-
boera. Un intermediario tedesco bendato
proveniente dalle linee boere viene
accompagnato per negoziare una resa,
17 marzo 1900.

Warriors all. British infantry, wearing pith helmets and the new khaki uniforms, charge a *kopje* with bayonets fixed, c. 1900. Although often posed especially for the camera, such pictures were good for morale at home.

"Los guerreros". La infantería británica, con típicos cascos coloniales y nuevos uniformes de color caqui, carga con bayonetas contra una pequeña colina aislada, hacia 1900. Los soldados posaban a menudo para la cámara, pues estas fotos estimulaban la moral de los que estaban en casa.

Tutti guerrieri. La fanteria britannica, con i caschi coloniali e le nuove uniformi color kaki, assaltano un *kopje* (piccola collina) baionetta in mano, ca. 1900. Anche se spesso i soldati apparivano chiaramente in posa, questo tipo di fotografie alzava il morale dei compatrioti in Gran Bretagna.

The backbone of Boer resistance – Afrikaaners in their farming clothes, armed with bolt action rifles, c. 1900.

El núcleo de la resistencia bóer. Afrikáners con sus ropas de campesino y armados con fusiles de palanca, hacia 1900.

L'intrepida resistenza boera. Afrikaner in borghese, con fucili a caricamento manuale, ca. 1900.

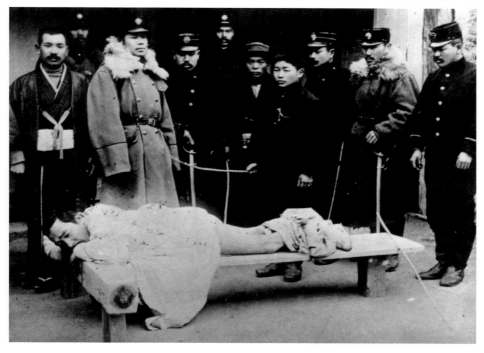

Neither photographers nor their clients were squeamish in the early 20th century. (Opposite) The public execution of one of the leaders of the Boxer Rebellion in China, 1900. (Above) Japanese troops beat a Korean prisoner to force a confession from him, 1905.

A principios del siglo XX, ni los fotógrafos ni sus clientes se horrorizaban fácilmente. (Página anterior) Ejecución pública de uno de los líderes de la Rebelión bóxer, en China, en 1900. (Arriba) Tropas japonesas golpean a un prisionero coreano para obligarle a confesar, 1905.

Agli inizi del XX secolo, né i fotografi né i loro clienti si facevano troppi scrupoli. (Pagina a fianco) Pubblica esecuzione di uno dei capi della Rivolta dei Boxer in Cina, 1900. (In alto) Truppe giapponesi torturano un prigioniero coreano per farlo confessare, 1905.

The streets of
Yokohama are
decorated to
celebrate a Japanese
victory in the war
with Russia, 1905.

Las calles
de Yokohama
decoradas para
celebrar una
victoria japonesa
en la guerra contra
Rusia, 1905.

Le strade di
Yokohama in festa
per celebrare la
vittoria giapponese
nella guerra contro
la Russia, 1905.

After the Battle of Port Arthur, the Russian battleship *Tsarevich* limps into Kinchan harbour, 10 August 1904. The surprise defeat of mighty Russia was greeted with approval by most Western countries.

Después de la batalla de Port Arthur, el buque de guerra ruso *Zarevich* entra lentamente en el puerto de Kinchan, el 10 de agosto de 1904. La sorprendente derrota de la poderosa Rusia fue acogida favorablemente por la mayoría de los países occidentales.

Dopo la battaglia di Port Arthur, la corazzata russa *Zarevich* avanza con difficoltà nelle acque del porto di Kinchan, 10 agosto 1904. La sconfitta inaspettata della potente Russia è ben accetta dalla maggior parte dei paesi occidentali.

The Russian rising
of 1905 was brutally
repressed by the
Tsar's troops and
police. The coffins
of some of those
killed are carried
through the streets.

La Revolución
rusa de 1905
fue brutalmente
reprimida por las
tropas y la policía
del zar. Los féretros
de algunas víctimas
son conducidos por
las calles de las
ciudades.

La rivoluzione
russa del 1905 fu
brutalmente repressa
dalle truppe e dalle
guardie dello zar.
Le salme di alcune
vittime sono portate
a spalla lungo le
strade del paese.

The *Potemkin*
mutiny, June 1905.
In the white shirt
is Matuchenko,
one of the leaders
of the uprising.

El motín del
Potemkin, en
junio de 1905.
El hombre de blanco
es Matuchenko, uno
de los líderes de la
rebelión.

L'ammutinamento
sulla corazzata
Potemkin, giugno
1905. Il personaggio
al centro con la
maglia bianca è
Matuchenko, uno
dei capi della rivolta.

After their failure to inspire a mutiny throughout the Russian fleet, members of the crew of the battleship *Potemkin* sought political asylum in the Romanian port of Constanta, 22 July 1905. They were favourably received.

Tras fracasar en su intento de provocar una rebelión en la flota rusa, miembros de la tripulación del acorazado *Potemkin* buscan asilo político en el puerto rumano de Constanta, donde son bien recibidos, 22 de julio de 1905.

Dopo il fallito tentativo di provocare una rivolta generale dell'armata russa, alcuni membri dell'equipaggio della corazzata *Potemkin* chiedono asilo politico in Romania. Il 22 luglio del 1905 giungono al porto di Constanta, dove sono accolti amichevolmente.

Official massacre. Bodies of Russian Jews killed during the rising of 1905 await burial in a cemetery. The suppression of the rising was used as an excuse to revile, persecute and slaughter many Jews.

Masacre oficial. Cuerpos de judíos rusos asesinados durante la revolución de 1905 esperan ser inhumados en un cementerio. La represión del levantamiento sirvió de pretexto para insultar, perseguir y asesinar a numerosos judíos.

Massacro ufficiale. I cadaveri degli ebrei russi uccisi durante la rivoluzione del 1905 prima di essere trasportati ad un cimitero. Con il pretesto di schiacciare la rivoluzione, molti ebrei furono umiliati, perseguiti e massacrati.

Mob rule. The body of Louis Higgins hangs from a bridge in Texas after he had been lynched in the summer of 1907.

La ley más salvaje. El cuerpo de Louis Higgins cuelga de un puente en Texas tras ser linchado en el verano de 1907.

La legge della violenza. Il corpo di Louis Higgins pende da un ponte del Texas dopo il suo linciaggio nell'estate del 1907.

Women arrive to cast their votes for the first time in Wellington North, 1909.
Although New Zealand became the first country to allow women the right
to vote, sadly at the time events there had little effect on the rest of the world.

Varias mujeres acuden a votar por primera vez al colegio electoral de Wellington
North, en 1909. Nueva Zelanda fue el primer país que reconoció el derecho de
la mujer al voto, pero en aquella época, desafortunadamente, la noticia tuvo
poca repercusión en el resto del mundo.

Alcune donne votano per la prima volta a Wellington North, 1909. Fu la
Nuova Zelanda il primo paese a concedere il diritto al voto alle donne, ma
purtroppo all'epoca un evento del genere non aveva grandi ripercussioni nel
resto del mondo.

In Britain the battle had not yet been won. Lady Emmeline Pethick-Lawrence, one of the leaders of the suffragette movement, addresses a crowd in Trafalgar Square, London, 1908. She received a mixed reception.

En Gran Bretaña, la batalla aún no se había ganado. Lady Emmeline Pethick-Lawrence, una de las líderes del movimiento por el sufragio femenino, se dirige a una multitud poco entusiasta en Trafalgar Square, Londres, 1908.

In Gran Bretagna, la battaglia non era ancora vinta. Lady Emmeline Pethick-Lawrence, una delle principali figure del movimento delle suffragette, si rivolge alla folla a Trafalgar Square, Londra, 1908. Il pubblico sembra piuttosto incerto.

Emmeline Pankhurst
(left) and her
daughter Christabel,
founders of the
Women's Social
and Political Union,
in prison clothes,
21 October 1908.

Emmeline Pankhurst
(izquierda) y su
hija Christabel,
fundadoras de
la Unión Social
y Política de
Mujeres, con
ropa de presidiarias,
21 de octubre
de 1908.

Emmeline Pankhurst
(a sinistra) e la figlia
Christabel, fondatrici
dell'Unione sociale e
politica delle donne,
con l'uniforme
carceraria,
21 ottobre 1908.

Anti-suffragette propaganda. The beautiful (and therefore apolitical) Mary Pickford laughingly reads a suffragette news sheet of 1909.

Propaganda antisufragista. La bella (y probablemente apolítica) Mary Pickford sonríe mientras lee un periódico de tendencia sufragista, 1909.

Propaganda contro le suffragette. La bellissima (e quindi apolitica) Mary Pickford sorride leggendo un giornale rivendicativo suffragista del 1909.

French police assault a striking worker as he leaves a meeting in the St Paul district of Paris, c. 1909. There was considerable industrial unrest throughout Europe at this time, and similar police harassment in most countries.

La policía francesa golpea a un obrero en huelga que sale de una reunión clandestina, en el barrio de St. Paul, hacia 1909. En aquella época hubo muchos disturbios obreros en toda Europa, y en la mayoría de los países la policía actuaba violentamente para reprimirlos.

La polizia francese aggredisce un lavoratore in sciopero mentre abbandona una riunione nel quartiere parigino di Saint-Paul, ca. 1909. All'epoca, l'agitazione sociale era molto diffusa in tutta Europa ed era possibile assistere a una scena simile in qualsiasi paese.

A group of unemployed demonstrate for the right to work, London, 1 October 1908. The banner reads 'Work or Riot – One or the Other'. It was a bold and criminal slogan, which could have earned all of them a spell in gaol.

Un grupo de parados en una manifestación por el derecho al trabajo, Londres, 1 de octubre de 1908. La pancarta dice: "Trabajo o revolución. Una de dos". Un eslogan tan provocador podía llevarles a la cárcel a todos.

Un gruppo di disoccupati manifestano a Londra per il diritto al lavoro, 1º ottobre 1908. Sullo striscione si legge "Lavoro o rivolta – Una cosa o l'altra". Uno slogan temerario e illegale che avrebbe potuto farli finire tutti in prigione per un po'.

3. Peoples
Gentes
Popoli

Spencer Arnold's photograph of a young Sinhalese girl in 1900. By then, the camera had done much to familiarise Westerners with their fellow human beings from all over the world, though many still viewed them as curiosities.

Fotografía de Spencer Arnold de una joven cingalesa en 1900. Por aquel entonces, la cámara había hecho un gran trabajo para familiarizar a los occidentales con el resto de sus congéneres en todo el mundo, pero muchos aún los veían como una curiosidad.

Fotografia di Spencer Arnold: una giovane ragazza singalese nel 1900. All'epoca, la macchina fotografica aveva già permesso agli occidentali di familiarizzarsi con i loro parenti di ogni parte del mondo, ma erano ancora in molti a vederli come una curiosità.

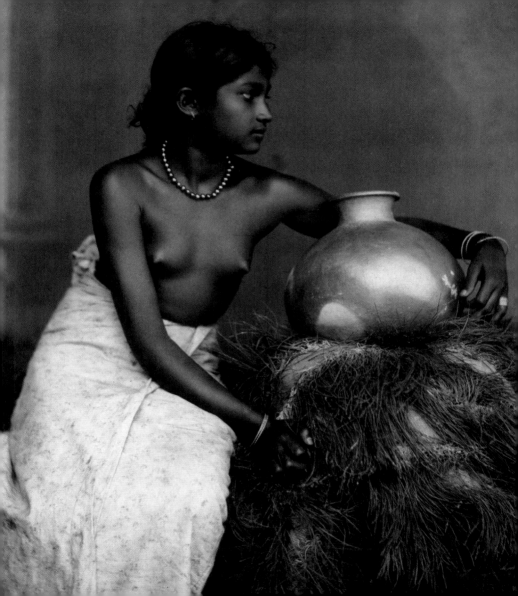

3. Peoples
Gentes
Popoli

For a while it seemed possible that the inhabitants of the world might lose their fear of each other. The railway and the steamship had brought the exotic within comparatively easy reach, and even the poor became familiar with their opposite numbers from the other side of the globe as immigrant workers poured into Western Europe and the United States. But 'foreigners' were still regarded with suspicion and were looked upon as oddities, freaks and delinquents by many of the Christian West.

At best, Westerners viewed the inhabitants of far-flung continents as quaint, though there were plenty who were moved by portraits of dusky maidens or young African warriors in ways that Dr Sigmund Freud was just beginning to reveal. The notion that people in the northern latitudes were somehow superior to those of the tropics was firmly established in many minds, and 'Hottentots' were unfavourably compared with 'Eskimos'. The former were charming but idle; the latter were plain but industrious.

And yet, forcing its way through this barrier of prejudice and racism was a new breed of scientists. Émile Durkheim's methods of examining societies, pioneered in the early 1900s, were seized upon by anthropologists. The world was coming into sharper focus.

Por un instante pareció que todos los habitantes del planeta podían perder el miedo que se profesaban mutuamente. El ferrocarril y los barcos de vapor habían permitido que lo exótico estuviera algo más cerca, e incluso los pobres se familiarizaron con sus homónimos de otras regiones del planeta, sobre todo gracias a las masas de obreros inmigrantes que llegaban a Estados Unidos y Europa occidental. Sin embargo, los "extranjeros" aún eran vistos con recelo y se les consideraba extraños, inadaptados o delincuentes en la mayor parte del Occidente cristiano.

En el mejor de los casos, los occidentales veían a los habitantes de tan lejanos continentes como seres pintorescos, aunque muchos, y el doctor Sigmund Freud estaba empezando a comprender por qué, se sentían atraídos por las muchachas de color o los jóvenes guerreros africanos que veían en las fotos. La idea de que los habitantes de las latitudes altas eran de una forma u otra superiores a las gentes de las zonas tropicales estaba ampliamente aceptada, con lo que los hotentotes, por ejemplo, recibían un trato desigual al compararlos con los esquimales. Los primeros eran simpáticos pero holgazanes, mientras que los segundos eran vulgares pero trabajadores.

Para los científicos, sin embargo, el muro de prejuicios y racismo constituía un nuevo objeto de estudio. Así, los antropólogos adoptaron los métodos de análisis de la sociedad creados por Émile Durkheim a principios del siglo XX. El mundo comenzaba a comprenderse de verdad.

Per un po' di tempo, sembrava quasi che tutti gli abitanti del pianeta avrebbero potuto perdere le paure che provavano nei confronti degli altri. I treni e le navi a vapore riducevano le distanze rispetto ai paesi esotici e perfino i meno ricchi potevano entrare in contatto con i loro omologhi dell'altra parte del mondo: migliaia di immigranti giungevano in Europa occidentale e negli Stati Uniti in cerca di lavoro. Ma questi "forestieri" erano ancora guardati con sospetto nell'occidente cristiano, degli esseri strambi, e magari dei delinquenti.

Nel migliore dei casi, gli occidentali consideravano gli abitanti di questi vastissimi paesi come un qualcosa di pittoresco, ma erano in molti ad essere attratti dai ritratti di oscure donzelle o di giovani guerrieri africani, con sentimenti che il dottor Sigmund Freud iniziava allora a rivelare. Convinti che i popoli del nord fossero in un certo qual modo superiori a quelli dei tropici, preferivano gli eschimesi, semplici ma industriosi, agli ottentotti, affascinanti ma indolenti.

Malgrado tutto, una nuova generazione di scienziati si faceva strada tra questa selva di pregiudizi razziali. Agli inizi del Novecento, Émile Durkheim pubblicava i primi metodi di ricerca sociologica, subito adottati dagli antropologi. L'immagine del mondo diventava più nitida.

Few realised at the
time that the camera
was recording
vanishing civilisations.
The early 20th century
had little respect for
other cultures.

En aquella época,
pocos se daban cuenta
de que la cámara
filmaba civilizaciones a
punto de desaparecer.
Los primeros años del
siglo XX tuvieron poco
respeto por otras
culturas.

Fotografie di popoli
in via di estinzione;
all'epoca, quasi
nessuno ci pensava.
I primi anni del
XX secolo portavano
poco rispetto verso
le altre culture.

(Opposite) A Maori
man in ceremonial
robes, 1900.
(Right) A Maori
woman on the porch
of an elaborately
decorated house.

(Página anterior)
Un hombre maorí
con sus atuendos
ceremoniales, 1900.
(Derecha) Una
mujer maorí en el
porche de una casa
con una decoración
muy elaborada.

(Pagina a fianco)
Un maori in abiti
da cerimonia, 1900.
(A destra) Una
maori sulla veranda
di una casa ricca di
decorazioni.

A young girl from
the north-east
Indian state of
Manipur carrying
a large umbrella.

Una joven del estado
de Manipur, al
noreste de la India,
con un gran
paraguas.

Una ragazzina
indiana con in mano
un grande ombrello,
nello stato
nordorientale
di Manipur.

A Hindu fakir and other holy men from the city of Benares, on the River Ganges, 1909. Of all Britain's colonies, India was the most prized, the 'jewel in the crown', a land large enough to maintain much of its own culture.

Un faquir hindú y otros hombres santos de la ciudad de Benarés, junto al río Ganges, en 1909. De todas las colonias británicas, la India era la más preciada, la "joya de la corona", una región lo suficientemente extensa como para conservar casi intacta su propia cultura.

Un fachiro indù con altri santoni della città di Varanasi, sulle rive del Gange, 1909. Di tutte le colonie britanniche, l'India era la più pregiata, il "gioiello della corona", un territorio abbastanza vasto da poter mantenere le proprie tradizioni culturali.

Wherever they lived, European Jews preserved their way of life, their culture and their language – though they were often persecuted and driven from their homes in the pogroms of Eastern Europe. Here Polish Jews pose for the camera, c. 1900.

Dondequiera que viviesen, los judíos europeos conservaban su forma de vida, su cultura y su idioma, a pesar de sufrir persecuciones y expulsiones durante los frecuentes pogromos ocurridos en Europa oriental. En la imagen, judíos polacos posan ante la cámara, hacia 1900.

Dovunque si stabilissero, gli ebrei d'Europa preservavano il loro stile di vita, la cultura e la lingua – anche se spesso dovevano subire persecuzioni e pogrom nell'Europa orientale. Ebrei polacchi in posa, ca. 1900.

Traditional ways of life included traditional ways of earning a living. Few worked harder than the women of the ancient Copenhagen fish market, Denmark, 1906. Food supply to big cities was still largely in the hands of individuals.

Las formas de vida tradicionales conservaban los oficios tradicionales. Pocos trabajaban más que las mujeres del antiguo mercado de pescado de Copenhague, Dinamarca, en 1906. El suministro de alimentos a las grandes ciudades dependía aún de unas pocas personas.

Uno stile di vita tradizionale comporta un modo tradizionale di guadagnarsi la vita. Uno dei lavori più pesanti, quello delle pescivendole del vecchio mercato di Copenhagen, Danimarca, 1906. Il rifornimento alimentare delle grandi città era ancora nelle mani dei singoli individui.

By the beginning of the 20th century, most Native Americans had been driven from their lands and forced to adopt the white man's ways.

A principios del siglo XX, la mayoría de los indios americanos habían sido expulsados de sus tierras y se habían visto obligados a adoptar la forma de vida del hombre blanco.

Ai primi del Novecento, la maggior parte delle popolazioni indigene d'America era stata scacciata dalle proprie terre e costretta ad adottare i costumi dell'uomo bianco.

Some – such as Show As He Goes (opposite) and this young Hopi mother and child (right) – were photographed by Edward S Curtis as part of a lasting record of a fast-disappearing culture.

Algunos indios americanos, como *El que muestra al avanzar* (página anterior) y esta joven madre de la tribu hopi y su hijo (derecha), fueron retratados por Edward S. Curtis, que inmortalizó los últimos momentos de una cultura a punto de desaparecer.

Alcune fotografie di Edward S. Curtis – come Show As He Goes (Mostra colui che parte) (pagina a fianco) e quella della giovane madre hopi con bambino (a destra) sono state scattate come testimonianze di culture in via d'estinzione.

Technically free. A generation after the abolition of slavery in
the United States, the average black American lived barely above
subsistence level. This family was photographed in Oklahoma
in 1901.

Presunta libertad. Una generación después de la abolición de la
esclavitud en Estados Unidos, el americano negro medio apenas
podía subsistir. Esta familia fue fotografiada en Oklahoma en 1901.

Libertà, in teoria. Una generazione dopo l'abolizione della
schiavitù, negli Stati Uniti i neri d'America sopravvivono a
stento. La fotografia di questa famiglia è stata scattata in
Oklahoma nel 1901.

Technologically enslaved. However bad life was for the black American, it was worse for the average African. Slavery and vicious cruelty were a way of life in many European colonies. (Above) A group of slaves is guarded by an Ashanti soldier.

Esclavitud tecnológica. Si la vida era difícil para el americano de color, para el africano medio era todavía peor. La esclavitud y los malos tratos eran una práctica habitual en muchas colonias europeas. (Arriba) Un grupo de esclavos custodiado por un soldado *ashanti*.

Schiavitù, in pratica. Per quanto fosse dura la vita dei neri americani, in Africa era ancora peggio. La schiavitù esisteva ancora in molte colonie europee, accompagnata da una malvagia crudeltà immorale. (In alto) Un gruppo di schiavi sorvegliato da un soldato ashanti.

A Old-style law. Headmen of the Tlingit tribe of the north-west coast of America. The elaborate blankets worn by two of the men, called Chilkat blankets, were traditionally woven from cedar bark and mountain goat's wool and would be worn for a potlatch.

Leyes ancestrales. Jefes de la tribu tlingit, en la costa noroeste de América. Las elaboradas mantas que llevan dos de ellos, llamadas *chilkat*, se tejían tradicionalmente con corteza de cedro y lana de cabra montesa y solían llevarse durante los *potlach*, fiestas en las que se intercambiaban obsequios.

La legge ancestrale. I capi della tribù Tlingit, della costa nordoccidentale d'America. Le coperte Chilkat che portano due di loro erano realizzate con corteccia di cedro e lana di capra di montagna, spesso con elaborati disegni, e indossate nei potlatch (feste di esibizione e distribuzione di ricchezza).

New-style law. Judge Henry H Campbell is master of all he surveys on the Matador Ranch, Texas, 1908 (photograph by Erwin E Smith). The problem was that much of what he surveyed was harsh scrubland, and even his own cabin was far from prepossessing.

Leyes modernas. El juez Henry H. Campbell era el propietario de todas las tierras que su vista podía alcanzar, en el rancho Matador, Texas, en 1908 (foto de Erwin E. Smith). Lo que ocurre es que casi todo eran tierras áridas y matorrales, y su propia cabaña no era precisamente muy lujosa.

La nuova legge. Il giudice Henry H. Campbell possiede tutto il territorio che può controllare a vista d'occhio, Matador Ranch, Texas, 1908 (fotografia di Erwin E. Smith). Il problema è che per la maggior parte si tratta di terra dura e sterile, e anche la sua dimora non fa certo una buona impressione.

There was little left of the world that was unexplored, but in the far north of the American continent there were still vast wildernesses of which little was known. These Canadian Native Americans of the Subarctic were trappers, hunters and fishermen.

Quedaban pocas regiones sin explorar en el planeta, pero en el extremo norte del continente americano aún había territorios vírgenes muy poco conocidos. Estos indios americanos de las regiones subárticas de Canadá eran tramperos, cazadores y pescadores.

Era rimasto ben poco da esplorare, ma all'estremo nord del continente americano c'erano ancora grandi spazi selvaggi e sconosciuti. Gli indiani della regione subartica del Canada erano trapper, cacciatori e pescatori.

Although this Alaskan hut of 1900 was said to be a great improvement on the more traditional dwellings of the indigenous natives of Yakutat Bay, the photographer noted: 'The dull, stupid or resigned look on their faces… appears to be the result of contact with civilisation.'

Esta cabaña de Alaska, en el año 1900, se consideraba mucho mejor que las viviendas tradicionales de los indígenas de Yakutat Bay. Sin embargo, el fotógrafo anotó: "La tristeza, estupidez o resignación que se refleja en sus caras … parece el resultado del contacto con la civilización".

Si diceva che in Alaska queste baracche rappresentassero un grande passo avanti rispetto alle dimore tradizionali dei nativi di Yakutat Bay. Nel 1900, il fotografo commentava: "Lo sguardo smorto, stupido o rassegnato sui loro volti… sembra piuttosto essere il risultato del contatto con la civilizzazione".

Little more than twenty years had passed since the war in which a British army had been annihilated by Zulu impis at Isandhlwana in 1879. Their teeth drawn, the Zulus shown here are almost certainly carrying ceremonial or dance regalia rather than weapons of war.

Poco más de 20 años después de la guerra en la que un ejército británico fue exterminado por guerreros zulús *impis* en Isandhlwana, en 1879, los zulús que aparecen en la imagen ya no llevan armas de guerra sino objetos ceremoniales o de danza.

Sono passati poco più di venti anni dalla guerra in cui un'armata britannica fu annientata dai guerrieri Zulu a Isandhlwana, nel 1879. Gli Zulu della fotografia quasi sicuramente si preparano per una cerimonia o una danza piuttosto che per una guerra.

In the wake of the armies of the West trudged the photographers, the anthropologists and the newly emerging social scientists. They recorded houses, tools, implements and – especially – people, such as these young Zulu women of 1900.

Fotógrafos, antropólogos y nuevos científicos sociales se contaban entre las filas de los ejércitos occidentales. Fotografiaban casas, herramientas, instrumentos y, sobre todo, a la gente, como estas jóvenes zulús, 1900.

Sulla scia degli eserciti delle potenze occidentali arrancavano fotografi, antropologi e i novelli sociologi, con il compito di studiare le case, gli arnesi, gli utensili e soprattutto la gente, come queste due giovani Zulu in un'immagine del 1900.

4. Migration
Migraciones
Migrazioni

Beset with a mixture of hope, anxiety and bewilderment, a young immigrant arrives at Ellis Island, New York, in 1905. By this time more than 100,000 religious, political and economic refugees were sailing from Europe to the United States every year.

Sumido en una mezcla de esperanza, angustia y desconcierto, un joven inmigrante desembarca en Ellis Island, Nueva York, en 1905. En esa época, cada año más de 100.000 refugiados políticos, religiosos o económicos dejaban Europa para ir a Estados Unidos.

Piena di speranza, angoscia e smarrimento allo stesso tempo, una giovane emigrante giunge ad Ellis Island, New York, 1905. All'epoca, più di 100.000 rifugiati, per ragioni politiche, religiose o economiche, partivano dall'Europa ogni anno per raggiungere gli Stati Uniti.

4. Migration
Migraciones
Migrazioni

They came by ship – from China to California, from India to Africa, from Europe to the eastern seaboard of the United States. Few of them came of their own free will, for they were driven by desperation. They were desperate for freedom, work or both. They had heard of new lands and new opportunities, of cities where the old prejudices and bigotry did not exist, of virgin land unbroken by the plough. They had also heard of streets paved with gold, of earth so rich and fecund that crops grew from seed to maturity in the space of a few days, of rocks that spewed forth jewels and the ore of precious metals by the barrow-load.

Their courage matched their naïvety. They braved storms at sea in vessels scarcely strong enough to withstand the waves of thousands of miles of ocean. They risked the strong possibility of rejection at the end of their journeys and an immediate return to the land whence they came. For the lands that summoned the destitute and the homeless had no welcome for the physically frail or the politically unsound.

But still they came in their hundreds of thousands, becoming the new citizens of new nations, bringing with them old cultures, old skills and, in a few, sad cases, old prejudices.

Llegaron por mar. De China a California, de India a África, de Europa a la costa este de Estados Unidos. Pocos lo hacían libremente, pues les conducía la desesperación, el anhelo de encontrar libertad o trabajo, o ambas cosas. Habían oído hablar de un mundo nuevo y de nuevas oportunidades, de ciudades donde el fanatismo y los viejos prejuicios no tenían lugar, de tierras vírgenes que no conocían el arado. También habían oído hablar de calles pavimentadas de oro, de tierras tan ricas y fecundas que las cosechas crecían en cuestión de días, de rocas que expulsaban joyas y arenas llenas de minerales preciosos.

Verdaderamente, el coraje que mostraban no era inferior a su ingenuidad. A lo largo de miles de millas por el océano, soportaron terribles tormentas en embarcaciones que a duras penas resistían el embate de las olas, y se arriesgaron a ser rechazados al final del viaje y tener que regresar de inmediato a su tierra. El nuevo mundo que buscaban los indigentes y desheredados no aceptaba a los que eran físicamente débiles o políticamente sospechosos.

Sin embargo, seguían llegando a miles los que pronto se convertirían en ciudadanos de nuevos países. Con ellos traían su antigua cultura, sus conocimientos y, en algunos casos, también sus viejos prejuicios.

Arrivavano in nave – dalla Cina in California, dall'India in Africa, dall'Europa sulla costa orientale degli Stati Uniti. Erano in pochi a partire di loro spontanea volontà, la maggior parte erano spinti dalla disperazione. Disperati per mancanza di libertà, lavoro o entrambe le cose. Avevano sentito parlare di nuove terre e nuove opportunità, di città in cui i vecchi pregiudizi e l'intolleranza non esistevano, terre vergini in attesa di un aratro. E anche di strade asfaltate d'oro, di una terra così ricca e fertile che le sementi maturavano in pochi giorni, di miniere che vomitavano diamanti e metalli preziosi a non finire.

Quanto coraggio e quanta ingenuità. Affrontavano le tempeste marine su navi che resistevano a malapena alle onde per migliaia di chilometri attraverso l'oceano. Correvano anche il rischio di non essere accettati, con un'alta probabilità di essere rispediti a casa appena sbarcati. La terra promessa dei bisognosi e dei senzatetto non accoglieva di buon grado le persone di fragile costituzione o di idee politiche sbagliate.

Malgrado tutto, milioni di emigranti riuscivano a passare, nuovi cittadini di nuove nazioni, portando con loro antiche culture, antichi mestieri e purtroppo, in alcuni casi, anche antichi pregiudizi.

A Polish emigrant
boards the
SS *General Grant* –
the last leg in
a journey of hope
to the New World.

Un emigrante
polaco a bordo
del buque *General
Grant*, la última
etapa de un viaje
lleno de esperanzas
hacia el Nuevo
Mundo.

Un emigrante
polacco si imbarca
sulla nave a vapore
General Grant –
l'ultima tappa di un
viaggio di speranza
verso il Nuovo
Mondo.

Emigrants crowd together on the deck of the White Star Company liner *Westernland*, sailing from Antwerp to New York. Their journey may have begun months earlier, in a horse-drawn cart or on foot, trudging from east to west across Europe.

Emigrantes apiñados en la cubierta del transatlántico *Westernland* de la White Star Company en su viaje de Amberes a Nueva York. Es probable que su odisea comenzara meses atrás, a pie o en un carro de caballos, cruzando Europa de este a oeste.

Alcuni emigranti stipati sul ponte della *Westernland*, della compagnia White Star, in partenza da Anversa per New York. Sono in viaggio da mesi, hanno attraversato l'Europa, diretti ad ovest, a piedi o su un carro trainato da cavalli.

(Opposite)
Immigrants begin
the 'processing'
at Ellis Island.
(Right) An elderly
Jew gazes out at a
new Promised Land.

(Página anterior)
Inmigrantes a
punto de iniciar
los trámites en Ellis
Island. (Derecha)
Un viejo judío
contempla la nueva
Tierra Prometida.

(Pagina a fianco) Un
gruppo di emigranti
in attesa del
permesso di sbarco
ad Ellis Island. (A
destra) Un anziano
ebreo contempla
la nuova Terra
Promessa.

The Registry Hall on Ellis Island, 1905. Penned in like cattle, the immigrants waited for their numbers to be called. Their real names were often abandoned by officials unable to distinguish names from destinations as pronounced by the new arrivals.

La sala de registro de Ellis Island, en 1905. Encerrados como ganado, los inmigrantes esperan su turno. A veces se perdían sus nombres verdaderos debido a que los funcionarios no sabían distinguirlos de sus destinos cuando los recién llegados los pronunciaban.

La Sala di Registrazione di Ellis Island, 1905. In un recinto, come se di bestie si trattasse, gli immigrati attendevano di essere chiamati per numero. Spesso i funzionari americani modificavano i loro nomi, incapaci di distinguerli dai nomi del luogo di destinazione che i nuovi arrivati pronunciavano come potevano.

A customs official attaches labels to the coats of a German immigrant family in the Registry Hall, 1905. Most families managed to keep together, for there was no rush and no panic – only the dreadful fear of rejection and summary return to Europe.

Un funcionario de aduanas pega etiquetas en los abrigos de una familia de inmigrantes alemanes en la sala de registro, en 1905. La mayoría de las familias conseguían mantenerse juntas, pues no solía haber prisas ni alborotos, pero les atenazaba el miedo de ser rechazados y devueltos a Europa.

Un funzionario della dogana attacca delle etichette sui cappotti di una famiglia di immigrati tedeschi nella Sala di Registrazione, 1905. La maggior parte delle famiglie riuscivano a restare unite, perché non c'era nessuna fretta – solo la paura terribile di essere respinti e subito rimpatriati.

The moment of truth – new immigrants are inspected for signs of disease, c. 1900. Fail this test and there was no hope of entry into the United States.

El momento de la verdad. Nuevos inmigrantes en un control para detectar posibles enfermedades, hacia 1900. Si no lo superaban, perdían toda esperanza de entrar en Estados Unidos.

Il momento della verità: il controllo sanitario, ca. 1900. Se non si superava questa prova cadeva ogni speranza di poter entrare negli Stati Uniti.

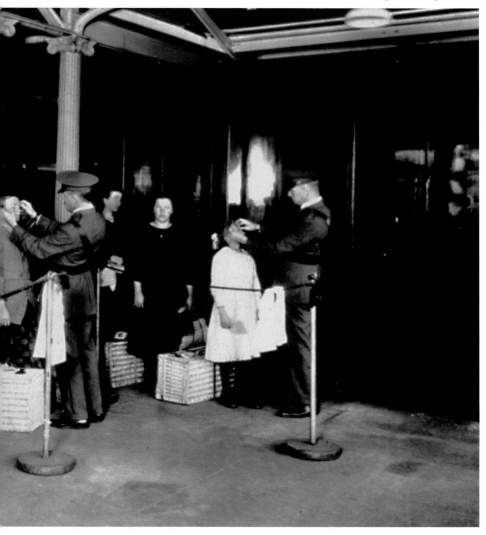

Jewish emigrants from England await inspection at Ellis Island, c. 1900. There were two doors leading from the main building. One led to boats for the short crossing to New York City. The other – for the unsuccessful – led to ships for the long journey back to Europe.

Emigrantes judíos de Inglaterra esperan ser inspeccionados en Ellis Island, hacia 1900. El edificio principal tenía dos puertas de salida. Una llevaba a los barcos que cubrían el corto trayecto hasta la ciudad de Nueva York. La otra, para quienes no eran aceptados, conducía a los barcos que realizaban el largo viaje de vuelta a Europa.

Emigranti ebrei provenienti dall'Inghilterra in attesa dell'ispezione ad Ellis Island, ca. 1900. L'edificio principale aveva due porte di accesso. Una conduceva al traghetto che attraversava il breve tratto tra l'isola e New York. L'altra, per i meno fortunati, portava alle navi pronte ad affrontare il lungo viaggio di ritorno per l'Europa.

Jakob Mithelstadt, his wife and family, newly arrived from Russia on the SS *Pretoria*, await permission to proceed to Kulm, North Dakota. Often, immigrants arrived with a single name scribbled on a piece of paper. Sometimes it was their own, sometimes that of their destination.

Jakob Mithelstadt, su esposa y sus hijos, recién llegados de Rusia en el buque *Pretoria*, esperan permiso para viajar hasta Kulm, en Dakota del Norte. A menudo, los inmigrantes llegaban con un simple nombre escrito en un trozo de papel. Unas veces era su nombre; otras, el de su lugar de destino.

Jakob Mithelstadt, sua moglie e i loro figli, appena giunti dalla Russia sulla nave a vapore *Pretoria*, in attesa del permesso per dirigersi a Kulm, nel Dakota del nord. Spesso gli immigranti portavano con sé un pezzo di carta su cui avevano scarabocchiato un nome, a volte il loro e a volte quello del luogo di destinazione.

A group of Italian immigrants in the waiting hall at Ellis Island. Most Italians headed straight for New York, Chicago or another large city. There was plenty of work in the sweatshops of New York's Little Italy.

Un grupo de inmigrantes italianos en la sala de espera de Ellis Island. La mayoría de los italianos se dirigían directamente a Nueva York, Chicago u otras grandes ciudades. Había mucho trabajo, aunque en condiciones de explotación, en el barrio neoyorquino de Little Italy.

Un gruppo di emigranti italiani nel salone d'attesa ad Ellis Island. La maggior parte degli italiani si dirigeva direttamente a New York, Chicago o altre grandi città. Non era difficile trovare un lavoro, seppure duro e malpagato, nel quartiere newyorkese di Little Italy.

Italian immigrants
at Ellis Island, 1905.
It is unlikely that
the luggage in the
background belongs
to them.

Inmigrantes italianos
en Ellis Island, en
1905. Es poco
probable que el
equipaje que tienen
detrás sea el suyo.

Emigranti italiani a
Ellis Island, 1905.
È poco probabile
che i bagagli alle
loro spalle
appartengano
a loro.

The pushcart market in the East Side ghetto of New York, 1900. This was the centre of the Jewish quarter. Newly-arrived Jews headed here for the newspaper offices which served as property and employment agencies and marriage bureaux.

Un mercado en el gueto del East Side neoyorquino, centro del barrio judío, en 1900. Los judíos recién llegados acudían a las oficinas de prensa de esta zona, que funcionaban como agencias inmobiliarias, de empleo y matrimoniales.

I carretti a mano del mercato nel ghetto dell'East Side, New York, 1900. Era il centro del quartiere ebreo. Gli ebrei appena arrivati venivano subito qui, nelle sedi dei giornali che fungevano anche da agenzie immobiliari, di collocamento e matrimoniali.

An immigrant family in a New York slum, 1900. After a journey of several thousand miles, this one-room hovel was their new home. It was also the beginning of a new life, and, it was to be hoped, an end to persecution.

Familia de inmigrantes en un barrio bajo de Nueva York, en 1900. Tras un viaje de miles de kilómetros, esta pequeña casucha constituía su nuevo hogar, el principio de una nueva vida y, con un poco de suerte, el fin de las persecuciones.

Una famiglia di immigrati in un tugurio di New York, 1900. Dopo un viaggio di migliaia di chilometri, questa misera stanza era la loro nuova dimora. Era anche il punto di partenza per una nuova vita lontano dalle persecuzioni, come c'era da aspettarsi.

5. Haves and have-nots
Ricos y pobres
Ricchi e poveri

Rich and poor were united in their attitudes to taxation. The rich had been assaulted and insulted by the death duties imposed by the Liberal Government on large estates; the poor were more concerned with the threatened bread tax at the end of the decade.

Ricos y pobres compartían su rechazo a los impuestos. Los ricos se sentían agredidos e insultados por los fuertes impuestos sobre los grandes patrimonios aplicados por el gobierno liberal, mientras que los pobres estaban más preocupados por el impuesto sobre el pan que les amenazaba hacia finales de la década.

I ricchi ed i poveri avevano in comune l'atteggiamento nei confronti delle tasse. I ricchi si sentivano aggrediti ed insultati dall'imposizione brutale delle tasse di successione decretate dal governo liberale sulle grandi fortune; i poveri erano più preoccupati dalla tassa sul pane che li minacciava verso la fine del primo decennio del secolo.

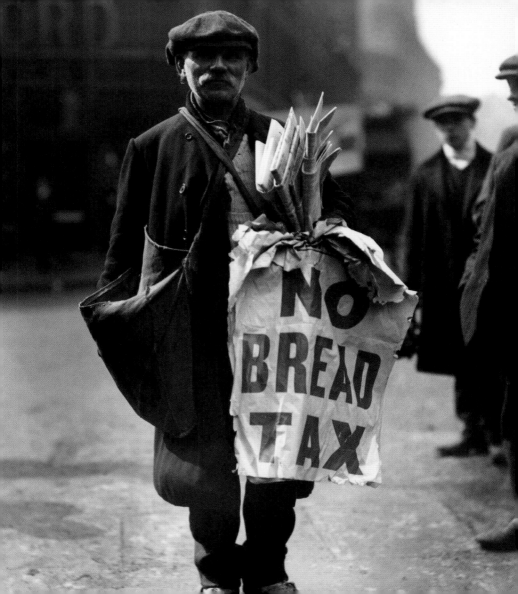

5. Haves and have-nots
Ricos y pobres
Ricchi e poveri

It is temptingly easy to romanticise the past, to exaggerate the quality of life of both rich and poor in the 1900s. Certainly, the poor were often ill-housed, ill-fed or just plain ill, but their lives were in many ways considerably better than they had been 50 or 60 years earlier. In all but the newest industrial nations there was legislation to limit hours of work and the worst excesses of exploitation. There were inspectors of factories and mines. There were bodies empowered to check the purity of the public water supply, to oversee education for all, to exercise some control over town and city development.

For all that, the poor still suffered extreme hardship. Social welfare schemes were in their infancy. Private charities offered patchwork care. It was hard for do-gooders to keep pace with the brash inventiveness of exploitation. There was little to stop the publican watering the workers' beer, the grocer from falsifying his scales, the landlord from overcrowding his slum tenements.

And, for all that, the rich did live in luxury and style beyond imagination. There was precious little room on the ladder that led from one class to another.

Es fácil y tentador idealizar el pasado y exagerar la calidad de vida que tenían ricos y pobres a principios del siglo XX. Ciertamente, las casas y la alimentación de los pobres dejaba mucho que desear, y su salud a menudo se resentía por ello, pero sus vidas eran mucho mejores que 50 o 60 años atrás. En todos los países salvo en los industrializados, las leyes limitaban la duración de la jornada laboral y prohibían los excesos de la explotación. Además de inspectores de fábricas y minas, había organismos encargados de comprobar la pureza del suministro público de agua, velar por que la educación llegara a todo el mundo, y controlar el crecimiento de pueblos y ciudades.

Sin embargo, los pobres seguían viviendo en unas condiciones muy duras. Los programas de asistencia social aún no habían nacido, y los centros de caridad privados solo podrían ofrecer ayudas transitorias. Los filántropos apenas podían competir con la insolente imaginación de los explotadores. Poco podía hacerse para impedir que el tabernero añadiera agua a la cerveza de los obreros o que el tendero hiciera trampa con el peso, o para que el amo proporcionara una vivienda digna a sus trabajadores.

Así pues, no debe extrañarnos que los ricos vivieran en un mundo de lujo y elegancia sin límites, y en la escalera que llevaba de una clase social a otra no había sitio para muchos.

È troppo facile cadere nella tentazione di idealizzare il passato, di esagerare sulla qualità di vita dei ricchi e dei poveri nel primo decennio del XX secolo. Senza dubbio i poveri erano spesso male alloggiati, malnutriti o malati, ma le condizioni di vita erano migliorate moltissimo per loro, rispetto a 50 o 60 anni prima. In quasi tutte le nazioni, eccetto quelle da poco industrializzate, la legislazione poneva limiti alle ore di lavoro e agli eccessi dello sfruttamento. C'erano ispettori nelle fabbriche e nelle miniere, istituzioni che controllavano la qualità del rifornimento idrico, assicuravano a tutti l'istruzione, cercavano di tenere sotto controllo le città ed il loro sviluppo.

Malgrado tutto, i poveri conducevano ancora una vita piena di stenti. L'assistenza sociale era ancora agli inizi e gli istituti di beneficenza non potevano raggiungere tutti. Per un buon samaritano era difficile far fronte alla sfacciata fantasia degli sfruttatori. C'era ben poco da fare se il locandiere annacquava la birra dei lavoratori, se il droghiere truccava la bilancia, se il padrone di casa stipava inverosimilmente le sue sudicie catapecchie.

E, malgrado tutto, i ricchi vivevano nel lusso più sfrenato. C'era poco spazio sulla scala che conduceva da una classe all'altra, ed erano in troppi ad ambirlo.

Families were often thrown out onto the street with their possessions. Eviction, in London and elsewhere, was a common fate and a constant nightmare for those who were unable to pay their rent. Casual workers – dockers, labourers and the unskilled – were the worst hit.

A menudo, las familias eran arrojadas a la calle con sus pertenencias. En Londres y en todas partes, el desahucio era una práctica habitual y una constante pesadilla para quienes no podían pagar el alquiler. Los temporeros, como los obreros portuarios, los jornaleros y los trabajadores sin oficio, eran los más afectados.

Spesso intere famiglie venivano buttate in strada con tutto quel che avevano. A Londra, e anche altrove, gli sfratti erano molto frequenti, un incubo costante per chi non poteva permettersi di pagare l'affitto. I lavoratori occasionali – scaricatori di porto, braccianti e operai non qualificati – erano i più colpiti.

Home was often a single room where all the family lived, worked and sometimes died. The luxury of a weekly bath from a basin by the fire was denied many; most went to the public baths or remained dirty.

Con frecuencia, el hogar se reducía a una sola habitación donde la familia entera vivía, trabajaba y a veces moría. El lujo de un baño semanal junto al fuego les estaba negado a muchos, y la mayoría acudía a los baños públicos o no se lavaba.

Le case erano spesso composte da una sola stanza in cui l'intera famiglia viveva, lavorava e a volte moriva. Un bagno settimanale in un catino vicino al fuoco era un lusso che non tutti potevano permettersi; la maggior parte andava ai bagni pubblici o non si lavava affatto.

In a life that threatened to be eaten away by misery, there were few means of escape. One (opposite) was a shot of morphine. Another – cheaper and longer lasting – was sleep. (Above) Vagrants doze on a bench in St James's Park, London, October 1900.

En una vida amenazada constantemente por la miseria, había pocas formas de evadirse. Una de ellas (página anterior) era la morfina. Otra, más barata y duradera, era dormir. (Arriba) Vagabundos durmiendo en un banco en St. James's Park, Londres, octubre de 1900.

Una vita rosa dalla miseria e poche scappatoie. Una di queste era la morfina (pagina a fianco). Un'altra, meno cara e più duratura, era il sonno. (In alto) Due vagabondi schiacciano un pisolino su una panchina del St. James's Park di Londra, ottobre 1900.

A few streets away life could be immeasurably better. Even a moderate income was enough for a large house, servants, holidays at the seaside, and a walled garden. This Edwardian family enjoys the garden in the summer of 1905.

A pocas calles de distancia, la vida podía ser infinitamente mejor. Incluso un nivel de ingresos medio podía ser suficiente para tener una casa grande, sirvientes, vacaciones en la playa y un pequeño jardín. Esta familia de la época de Eduardo VII disfruta de su jardín en el verano de 1905.

A poca distanza, la vita poteva essere di gran lunga migliore. Bastava un salario decente per potersi permettere una casa spaziosa, dei domestici, le vacanze al mare e un giardino protetto da alte mura. Sotto il regno di Edoardo VII, una famiglia si gode il suo giardino nell'estate del 1905.

This family, taking tea in 1909, is not particularly wealthy. The tablecloth is limp and slightly stained, and the children – despite their Eton collars – are not smartly dressed. But the ornaments, the bookshelves and the tea service indicate they are comfortable enough.

Esta familia que está tomando el té en 1909 no es especialmente rica. El mantel es viejo y está algo manchado, y los pequeños, a pesar de llevar cuellos duros, no van bien vestidos. Pero la decoración, las librerías y el servicio de té indican un cierto bienestar.

Una famiglia prende il tè, 1909. Non sono particolarmente ricchi: la tovaglia non è di buona qualità ed è anche macchiata e, malgrado i colletti inamidati, i bambini non sono ben vestiti. Ma l'arredamento, la libreria e il servizio da tè sono segnali di un certo benessere.

If you sought real comfort, it was better to be rich and male. However wealthy, a woman's place was in the home, a man's in his club. Hock and seltzer lads of the early 1900s meet to smoke and drink.

Para conseguir un buen nivel de vida, era preferible ser rico y varón. Aunque fuera rica, la mujer debía quedarse en casa, mientras que los hombres acostumbraban a ir al club. En la foto, un grupo de caballeros de principios de la década de 1900 reunidos para fumar y beber.

Per star bene veramente, era meglio essere ricchi e di sesso maschile. Una donna, per quanto ricca fosse, doveva stare in casa mentre l'uomo andava al club. Alcuni rappresentanti dell'alta società si riuniscono per fumare e bere agli inizi del XX secolo.

There were plenty of clubs for gentlemen, in town and country. Among the increasingly popular were sporting clubs. This is the 19th Hole at the fashionable Ranelagh Golf Club, near London, c. 1900.

Tanto en el campo como en la ciudad, había muchos clubes para caballeros. Los que gozaban de mayor popularidad eran los deportivos. En la foto, el hoyo 19 del moderno club de golf de Ranelagh, cerca de Londres, hacia 1900.

C'era un gran numero di club per gentiluomini, in città ed in campagna. I club sportivi erano sempre più di moda. Nella fotografia, la "19ª buca" del Ranelagh Golf Club vicino a Londra, ca. 1900.

A family in a London slum, 1901. Philanthropists throughout the West were doing what they could to improve housing for the poor, but the vast majority still lived in slums that were dark, dangerous, cold in winter and stifling in summer.

Una familia en un barrio pobre de Londres, en 1901. En toda Europa, los filántropos hacían lo posible para mejorar las condiciones de vida de los pobres, pero la gran mayoría de ellos aún vivía en suburbios oscuros y peligrosos, fríos en invierno y sofocantes en verano.

Una famiglia nel loro tugurio a Londra, 1901. I filantropi del mondo occidentale facevano del loro meglio per cercare di migliorare le condizioni dei più poveri, ma la maggior parte di loro viveva ancora in catapecchie buie, pericolose, fredde in inverno e soffocanti in estate.

An idyllic outing for all ages and both sexes – a picnic party at Netley Abbey, Hampshire, in the summer of 1900. The picnickers almost certainly travelled to the Abbey by horse-drawn charabanc.

Una idílica comida de campo para todas las edades y para ambos sexos. Tarde de *picnic* en Netley Abbey, Hampshire, en el verano de 1900. Con toda probabilidad, los asistentes llegaron a la abadía en un carro de caballos.

Idillica escursione per tutte le età ed entrambi i sessi: un picnic presso Netley Abbey, Hampshire, nell'estate del 1900. Quasi sicuramente i partecipanti hanno raggiunto l'abbazia con una giardiniera, il tipo di carrozza allora in voga.

The claustrophobic clutter of the Victorian parlour gave way to the simpler lines of Edwardian furnishing (above). The responsibility for dusting every ornament and every shelf – as well as a hundred other jobs – fell on the maid (opposite).

El claustrofóbico desorden de los salones victorianos dio paso a la simplicidad de las líneas del mobiliario eduardiano (arriba). La tarea de quitar el polvo de ornamentos y estanterías, entre otras mil tareas, recaía en la sirvienta (página siguiente).

Gli arredamenti claustrofobici dei salottini vittoriani lasciano spazio alle linee più semplici dell'epoca di Edoardo VII (in alto). Le domestiche avevano l'incarico di spolverare tutti i soprammobili e tutti gli scaffali, oltre a un gran numero di altri compiti (pagina a fianco).

As well as free handouts of bread and soup, the unemployed and the homeless in New York could visit the Bowery Mission for free cups of coffee. This picture was taken in February 1908 – a time when the American economy was booming.

Además de recibir un poco de pan y sopa, los parados y los sin techo de Nueva York podían disfrutar de un café gratis en Bowery Mission. Esta foto fue tomada en febrero de 1908, un época en que la economía americana estaba en pleno crecimiento.

I disoccupati e i senzatetto di New York potevano recarsi alla Bowery Mission dove, oltre a un pezzo di pane e un po' di minestra, gli veniva offerta anche una tazza di caffè. La fotografia è del febbraio del 1908, un periodo splendido per l'economia americana.

Across the other side of the world, 'Grand Russians' – in this case merchants from Nijni-Novgorod – take tea, 29 August 1905. The surroundings may look a little sparse, but the tea set and the samovar are most impressive.

En el otro extremo del mundo, varios miembros de la clase acomodada rusa, en este caso mercaderes de Nijni-Novgorod, toman el té, 29 de agosto de 1905. El entorno puede parecer austero, pero el servicio de té y el samovar son impresionantes.

Dall'altra parte del mondo, i "grandi russi", in questo caso dei mercanti di Nijni-Novgorod, prendono il tè, 29 agosto 1905. La scena potrebbe sembrare un po' austera, ma il servizio da tè e il samovar sono di grande effetto.

Stuffed shirts. Friends and colleagues of Richmond Keele in their serried ranks at a dinner in his honour at the Café Royal, London, 20 October 1903. The amount of cutlery on the tables suggests they are in for a 'beano'.

Reunión de estirados. Amigos y colegas de Richmond Keele sentados ordenadamente durante una cena en su honor, en el Café Royal, Londres, el 20 de octubre de 1903. La gran cantidad de cubiertos parece indicar que la cena será larga.

Palloni gonfiati. Amici e colleghi di Richmond Keele a schiere serrate durante una cena in suo onore al Café Royal di Londra, 20 ottobre 1903. Le numerose posate sui tavoli preannunciano un grande banchetto.

Empty bellies. A couple of miles away, on the same night, the benches of the Salvation Army shelter for the homeless of Blackfriars would have been crowded. The poor were best kept off the streets, where they might have caused mischief.

Estómagos vacíos. A unos kilómetros de distancia, esa misma noche, los bancos del refugio del Ejército de Salvación para los sin techo, en Blackfriars, estaban a rebosar. Se evitaba que los pobres deambularan por las calles para que no cometieran fechorías.

A stomaco vuoto. Pochi chilometri più in là, la sera stessa, le panche dell'Esercito della Salvezza, rifugio dei senzatetto di Blackfriars, sono strapiene. Si cercava di tenere i poveri lontano dalle strade, per evitare eventuali disordini.

A meeting place for rich and poor. Paul Martin's photograph shows a bootblack polishing the shoes of a London gentleman, c. 1900. The plinth behind the bootblack suggests that the scene is somewhere in the City of London.

Lugar de encuentro de ricos y pobres. Esta foto de Paul Martin muestra un limpiabotas sacando brillo a los zapatos de un *gentleman* londinense, hacia 1900. La estructura metálica de la derecha indica que la imagen está tomada en algún lugar de la City londinense.

Un punto d'incontro per ricchi e poveri. Nella fotografia di Paul Martin: un lustrascarpe lucida le calzature di un gentleman londinese, ca. 1900. La struttura alle sue spalle fa pensare che la scena si svolga nella City di Londra.

And meanwhile, well to the east, a more humble bootblack cleans the shoes of a less smart customer. In an age when there was far more mud and dust on the city streets, shoes needed cleaning more often than they do today.

Mientras, en algún lugar más al este, un limpiabotas más humilde limpia los zapatos de un cliente menos elegante. En una época en que las calles de las ciudades eran más polvorientas, los zapatos tenían que limpiarse más a menudo que en la actualidad.

Nel frattempo, ben più ad est, un lustrascarpe molto più umile lucida le calzature di un cliente molto meno elegante. In un'epoca in cui le strade delle città erano piene di fango e polvere, era necessario pulire le scarpe con maggior frequenza rispetto ad oggi.

6. Work
Trabajo
Lavoro

It was the last great age of coal. Coal powered factories, ships and railways, gave up its gas for fires and lighting, and drove the turbines and generators producing electricity. French miners, deep underground, 1909.

La era del carbón estaba a punto de terminar. Fábricas, barcos y trenes dependían de este combustible, que también se utilizaba en las cocinas y para iluminar, así como para mover las turbinas que producían electricidad. En la foto, mineros franceses bajo tierra, 1909.

Era l'ultima, grande epoca del carbone, una materia prima che alimentava le fabbriche, le navi ed i treni, provvedeva al riscaldamento e all'illuminazione e faceva girare le turbine ed i generatori che fornivano l'energia elettrica. Minatori francesi nel profondo di un pozzo, 1909.

6. Work
Trabajo
Lavoro

It was not an age that believed in the wisdom of keeping a percentage of the workforce idle. At daybreak, across the world, people trudged through the gates of factories, collieries, foundries; through the doors of offices, shops and stores; into fields, forests and pastures.

When times were bad, they were locked out and gathered in groups small and large on the docksides, on street corners or at the factory gates – begging, praying and sometimes battling for work. Economic depression was not unknown, but it had yet to reach the acute and chronic levels that were to come later in the century. It was just as well. Few governments had much to offer by way of social security.

Others lived where they worked. Hundreds of thousands of men and women spent their lives in domestic service, as butlers, valets, cooks, gardeners, maids, footmen, coachmen and – increasingly – chauffeurs. Millions more worked at home – in the sweatshops of London, Berlin, Paris, New York, Madrid, St Petersburg and a thousand more cities; in dimly-lit rooms where they stitched and sewed; around tables where they assembled toys and cheap jewellery; and in their tiny gardens where they cut flowers and picked vegetables.

There was work for all – but fortune for so few.

Aquella lejana época no creía mucho en la importancia del ocio como estimulante de la productividad. A punta de día, en todo el mundo, millones de trabajadores se dirigían a las fábricas, minas y fundiciones, cruzaban la puerta de sus oficinas, tiendas o almacenes, o partían hacia campos, bosques y prados.

Si las cosas iban mal y no había trabajo, se reunían en grupos junto a los muelles, en las esquinas o a la entrada de las fábricas para pedir, suplicar y, a veces, exigir trabajo. Aunque había fases de depresión económica, aún no se habían alcanzado las profundas crisis crónicas que azotarían al nuevo siglo. Daba igual, pues pocos gobiernos eran capaces de ofrecer servicios sociales.

Algunos vivían en el mismo sitio donde trabajaban. Miles de hombres y mujeres realizaban tareas domésticas como criados, mayordomos, cocineros, jardineros, sirvientas, lacayos o cocheros y, cada vez más, como chóferes. Muchos otros trabajaban en sus casas, en talleres clandestinos de París, Berlín, Nueva York, Madrid, San Petersburgo y otras ciudades, y se pasaban el día cosiendo en habitaciones mal iluminadas, confeccionando juguetes o joyas sentados a una mesa, o recogiendo flores y verduras en sus pequeños huertos.

Había trabajo para todos, pero la suerte solo sonreía a unos pocos.

In quegli anni, i lavoratori non avevano certo del tempo libero a disposizione. All'alba, in tutto il mondo, fiumi di gente si trascinavano penosamente all'entrata delle fabbriche, delle miniere di carbone e delle fonderie; alle porte degli uffici, dei negozi e delle botteghe; nei campi, nei boschi e nei pascoli.

Nei periodi di recessione, venivano sbattuti fuori ed era frequente vedere gruppi più o meno numerosi di persone che si radunavano sulle banchine, agli angoli delle strade e alle porte delle fabbriche per mendicare, pregare e a volte battersi per un posto di lavoro. La depressione economica si faceva già sentire, anche se ancora non aveva raggiunto i livelli cronici ed acutissimi che avrebbero caratterizzato i decenni seguenti. Meglio così, pochi governi erano in grado di offrire un'assistenza sociale decente.

Erano in molti a dormire sul posto di lavoro. Centinaia di migliaia di uomini e di donne passavano l'intera vita al servizio dei più benestanti come maggiordomi, camerieri, cuochi, giardinieri, domestiche e domestici, cocchieri e, sempre in maggior numero, autisti. Milioni di persone lavoravano in casa, sfruttati e malpagati dalle aziende di Londra, Berlino, Parigi, New York, Madrid, San Pietroburgo ed altre centinaia di città; in piccole stanze poco illuminate a cucire e ricamare; intorno a tavoloni dove montavano giocattoli e oggetti di bigiotteria; e nei loro minuscoli giardini in cui coltivavano fiori ed ortaggi.

C'era lavoro per tutti, ma la fortuna baciava solo poche persone.

The cats and dogs meat man with some of his non-paying customers in a London street, 1900. The supervision of Public Health had improved to the point where at least some meat was declared unfit for human consumption.

Un vendedor de carne para perros y gatos, junto a uno de sus clientes que no pagaba nunca, en una calle de Londres, en 1900. El sistema público de sanidad había mejorado hasta el punto que algunas carnes se declararon no aptas para el consumo humano.

Un venditore di carne per cani e gatti con alcuni dei suoi clienti "insolventi" in una strada di Londra, 1900. I controlli sanitari erano migliorati, almeno fino al punto da proibire la vendita di alcuni tipi di carne dichiarata non adatta al consumo umano.

Fruit from Hampshire awaits despatch to Edinburgh, 1902. Fruit and vegetables were only available 'in season' at the beginning of the 20th century. The strawberry season was a short one – a few weeks in June and July.

Fruta procedente de Hampshire espera ser enviada a Edimburgo, 1902. A principios del siglo XX, solo podían comprarse frutas y verduras de temporada. La temporada de las fresas era muy corta, tan solo duraba unas semanas entre junio y julio.

Cesti di frutta dell'Hampshire in attesa di essere spediti a Edimburgo, 1902. All'inizio del XX secolo, sul mercato si trovavano solo frutta e verdure di stagione. Quella delle fragole era una stagione cortissima, poche settimane tra giugno e luglio.

A family of strawberry pickers enjoys a break from work in a Hampshire field, 1902. They were almost certainly local people. At other times of year there would be potatoes to dig, or watercress to pick. Much of the time, there would be no work at all.

Una familia de recolectores de fresas disfrutan de un descanso en un campo de Hampshire, 1902. Con toda probabilidad, eran gente de la región. En otras épocas del año recogían patatas o berros, pero la mayor parte del tiempo no tenían trabajo.

Una famiglia di braccianti durante il raccolto delle fragole si gode una pausa in un campo dell'Hampshire, 1902. Quasi sicuramente è gente del posto. In altre stagioni potevano raccogliere patate o agretti, ma per la maggior parte dell'anno non c'era affatto lavoro.

Grinding out a living on the city streets. (Opposite) Eugène Atget's albumen
portrait of a knife grinder in Paris, c. 1900. (Above) Paul Martin's photograph
of children gathered round a street organ, complete with monkeys, c. 1900.

Ganarse la vida en las calles de la ciudad. (Página anterior) Retrato a la albúmina
de Eugène Atget de un afilador de cuchillos, en París, hacia 1900. (Arriba) Foto
de Paul Martin: niños alrededor de un órgano callejero decorado con monos,
hacia 1900.

A ruota libera, guadagnandosi il pane per le strade della città. (Pagina a fianco)
Ritratto con procedimento all'albumina di Eugène Atget, raffigurante un arrotino
a Parigi, ca. 1900. (In alto) Fotografia di Paul Martin, dei bambini riuniti intorno
ad un suonatore ambulante e alle sue scimmie, ca. 1900.

Although laws had been passed preventing children from digging coal, there was still plenty for young lads in mines and collieries. (Opposite) Cleaning coal in Bargoed, South Wales. (Above) Unloading coal barges in St Petersburg, Russia, 1900.

Aunque las leyes prohibían que los menores extrajeran carbón, aún había muchos jóvenes que trabajaban en minas y pozos. (Página anterior) Limpiando carbón en Bargoed, al sur de Gales. (Arriba) Transporte de carretillas de carbón en San Petersburgo, Rusia, 1900.

Malgrado fossero state approvate delle leggi che vietavano lo sfruttamento minorile nei pozzi delle miniere di carbone, queste erano ancora piene di bambini e adolescenti. (Pagina a fianco) Pulizia del carbone a Bargoed, nel sud del Galles. (In alto) Trasporto del carbone sulle chiatte a San Pietroburgo, Russia, 1900.

Miners arrive at the foot of the shaft to begin their shift, 1900. They needed to get there speedily: they would be paid from the time they reached the coalface.

Mineros llegando al pie del pozo para el cambio de turno, en 1900. Debían apresurarse, pues su jornada comenzaba en el momento en que llegaban a la veta de carbón.

Dei minatori giungono in fondo al pozzo per iniziare il loro turno, 1900. Dovevano arrivare lì rapidamente: venivano pagati a partire da quando raggiungevano il fronte di abbattimento del carbone.

Some ten hours later, miners wait to go back to the surface at the end of their shift, Bargoed, South Wales. Young boys often helped shunt the coal wagons along the rails, or worked with the pit ponies.

Unas diez horas más tarde, los mineros esperan para regresar a la superficie, en Bargoed, en el sur de Gales. A menudo, los más jóvenes ayudaban a conducir las vagonetas por los raíles o trabajaban con los animales de carga.

Circa dieci ore più tardi, dei minatori attendono di esser riportati in superficie alla fine del turno, Bargoed, Galles del Sud. Spesso i più giovani aiutavano ad instradare i carrelli sulle rotaie o lavoravano con i cavallini da miniera.

Sacks of hops await collection from a Hampshire farm, 1902. In France, Germany, Belgium, Britain and the United States, beer was the working man's drink. It slaked his thirst and drowned some of his sorrows.

Sacos de lúpulo esperan ser cargados en una granja de Hampshire, en 1902. En Francia, Alemania, Bélgica, Gran Bretaña y Estados Unidos, la cerveza era la bebida de los trabajadores. Saciaba su sed y ahogaba algunas de sus penas.

Sacchi di luppolo in attesa di essere prelevati in un magazzino dell'Hampshire, 1902. In Francia, Germania, Belgio, Gran Bretagna e Stati Uniti, la birra era la bevanda ufficiale dei lavoratori. Spegneva la sete ed affogava i loro dispiaceri.

More casual work for the country labourer – packing hops at harvest time, 1902. This is one of many photographs by F J Mortimer, who recorded Hampshire life in the early 20th century.

Trabajo temporal para jornaleros agrícolas: recogida de lúpulo en el tiempo de la cosecha, 1902. Esta es una de las muchas fotos de F. J. Mortimer, que dejó constancia de la vida de Hampshire a principios del siglo XX.

Ancora del lavoro avventizio per i contadini. Dopo la raccolta, il luppolo viene messo nei sacchi, 1902. Questa è una delle numerose fotografie di F. J. Mortimer, che ha immortalato la vita quotidiana dell'Hampshire nei primi anni del XX secolo.

Hastening the harvest. Vegetables are forced under glass domes on a farm, 1908. There were always choice and expensive early crops for the rich in the cities or on local estates. Others had to wait a few weeks longer.

Acelerando la cosecha. Cultivo de verduras en cúpulas de vidrio en una granja, en 1908. Para los ricos siempre había una gran variedad de productos, tempranos y caros, ya fuera en la ciudad o en el campo. Otros tenían que esperar un poco más.

Maturazione accelerata. Gli ortaggi vengono messi sotto delle campane di vetro in un vivaio, 1908. Nelle città o nelle loro residenze estive, i più facoltosi potevano sempre scegliere quando mangiare le loro primizie preferite, anche se a un prezzo più alto. Gli altri dovevano aspettare ancora qualche settimana.

Preserving the vintage. Thousands of bottles of champagne bide
their time in the cellars at Reims, France, that have existed since
Roman times. Here the tiny bubbles formed that would later
delight and intoxicate their consumers.

Conservando la vendimia. Miles de botellas de champán esperan
su hora en las bodegas de Reims, Francia, que datan del tiempo de
los romanos. Aquí se forman las pequeñas burbujas que más tarde
deleitarán y embriagarán a sus consumidores.

Vendemmia sotto protezione. Migliaia di bottiglie di champagne
attendono il loro momento nelle cantine francesi di Reims,
risalenti ai tempi dell'antica Roma. È qui che si formano le
bollicine, fonte di gioia e di ebbrezza per i consumatori.

A stockier version of Eliza Doolittle. One of London's many flower sellers, Regent Street, 1900.

Una versión voluminosa de Eliza Doolittle. Una de las muchas floristas de Londres, Regent Street, 1900.

Una Eliza Doolittle un po' più in carne. Non era affatto difficile incontrare una fioraia ambulante a Londra, Regent Street, 1900.

Not long out of school, but already earning a living, a boy refreshes
himself with a glass of sherbet water, Cheapside, London, 1900.
It would have cost him a ha'penny – roughly a fifth of a modern pence.

Este chico, que hasta hacía poco iba a la escuela y ahora debía ganarse
la vida, se refresca con un vaso de limonada, Cheapside, Londres, 1900.
Le ha costado medio penique, unos 20 céntimos de hoy.

Appena finita la scuola, ma già si guadagna da vivere. Un ragazzo si
rinfresca con un bicchiere di acqua aromatizzata, Cheapside, Londra,
1900. Gli sarebbe costato un mezzo penny, circa 20 centesimi di oggi.

Chefs prepare for a busy shift in the kitchens of the Hotel Cecil in London's West End, 1900. The Cecil was a famous hotel where the rich and famous, discerning and demanding, stayed.

Chefs a punto de comenzar su turno de trabajo en las cocinas del Hotel Cecil, en el West End de Londres, en 1900. El Cecil era un conocido hotel frecuentado por una elite refinada y exigente de ricos y famosos.

I cuochi si preparano per un pesante turno nelle cucine dell'Hotel Cecil nel West End di Londra, 1900. Il Cecil era un celebre hotel frequentato da personaggi ricchi e famosi, dal palato raffinato e molto esigenti.

Women packers in a factory that produced syrups and bottled fruit, 1900. Although a greater variety of jobs was available for women, most were still employed as domestic servants.

Mujeres trabajando en una fábrica de botes de almíbar y fruta en conserva, 1900. Aunque había una gran diversidad de trabajos para las mujeres, la mayoría todavía se ocupaba principalmente del servicio doméstico.

Operaie in azione in una fabbrica di sciroppi e frutta in conserva, 1900. Sebbene avessero la possibilità di cercare un impiego in vari settori, la maggior parte delle donne lavoravano come domestiche.

Early NYPD Blues. Members of the
New York City Police Department
with their sergeant parade in uniform
before going out on patrol, c. 1900.
Their helmets appear to be in a
transitional stage between those
of the British and the modern
American policeman.

Los primeros policías de Nueva York.
Miembros del departamento de
policía de Nueva York y su sargento
forman uniformados antes de salir
a patrullar, hacia 1900. El casco que
llevan es un modelo de transición
entre el de la policía británica y el
de la policía americana actual.

Alle origini della serie "NYPD Blues".
Membri del Dipartimento di Polizia
di New York in riga davanti al
sergente prima di andar di pattuglia,
ca. 1900. Gli elmetti sembrano a metà
strada tra la versione inglese e quella
della polizia americana di oggi.

A team of firemen, somewhere in England, direct their hose at a fire inside
a building, 1909. Fire was an everyday hazard in the days of open hearths,
draughts and a wealth of combustible material.

Una brigada de bomberos, en algún lugar indeterminado de Inglaterra, apuntan
la manguera hacia un fuego en el interior de un edificio. Los fogones al aire libre
y la gran cantidad de materiales inflamables de aquella época hacían del fuego un
peligro diario.

Da qualche parte in Inghilterra, un gruppo di pompieri dirige una pompa verso
un edificio in fiamme, 1909. Il fuoco era un pericolo costante in un'epoca in cui
i camini non avevano valvole di sicurezza e i materiali combustibili abbondavano.

A team of horses, somewhere in the United States, provide the motive power for a steam-driven fire appliance. It must have been a fearsome sight – more frightening than the fire itself.

Una brigada de caballos, en algún lugar indeterminado de Estados Unidos, tira de un vehículo antiincendios a vapor, un extraño artefacto que producía casi más miedo que el propio fuego.

Da qualche parte negli Stati Uniti, dei cavalli fanno da motore per un apparato antincendio a vapore. Doveva essere una scena spaventosa, forse anche più di quella dell'incendio stesso.

Fire! in America, 1900

Russian convicts at work on the eastern section of the Trans-Siberian railway, 1900. It was completed in 1902, though it took another three years of inspection, protection and organisation before it opened.

Presos rusos trabajando en el sector oriental del ferrocarril transiberiano, en 1900. Aunque la línea se terminó en 1902, la inauguración se demoró tres años debido a las tareas de inspección, seguridad y organización.

Carcerati russi al lavoro nel settore occidentale della linea ferroviaria transiberiana, 1900. Fu completata nel 1902, ma ci vollero altri tre anni per ispezionare, proteggere ed organizzare il servizio prima dell'inaugurazione della linea.

Women operatives at their looms in the winding room of a Lancashire
cotton mill. The hours were long, the work was hard, but in good times
the money they earned raised the entire family's standard of living.

Operarias de los telares en la sala de bobinado de una fábrica de algodón
en Lancashire. Las jornadas se hacían eternas y el trabajo era duro, pero en
las buenas épocas ganaban suficiente dinero para subir el nivel de vida de
toda la familia.

Donne in azione sui telai nella sala per la bobinatura di uno stabilimento
tessile nel Lancashire. Le ore passavano lentamente ed il lavoro era duro,
ma nei tempi migliori i soldi che guadagnavano facevano incrementare il
livello di vita di tutte le loro famiglie.

Black cotton pickers
in the American
South, 1900.
Though slavery had
been abolished, the
pay barely kept body
and soul together.

Recolectores de
algodón negros en
el sur de Estados
Unidos, 1900.
Aunque se había
abolido la
esclavitud, su sueldo
apenas daba para
vivir.

Bambini di colore
raccolgono il cotone
nel sud degli Stati
Uniti, 1900.
Malgrado
l'abolizione della
schiavitù, con
i pochi soldi che
prendevano non
riuscivano quasi
a sopravvivere.

Workers folding and
starching linen in a
Belfast factory at the
turn of the century.
The production
of linen was a
staple industry of
Northern Ireland.

Obreros plegando
y almidonando piezas
de lino en una fábrica
de Belfast a principios
del siglo XX. La
producción de
lino era una de las
principales industrias
de Irlanda del Norte.

Due operai piegano
il lino e lo apprettano
in una fabbrica di
Belfast agli inizi del
secolo. La produzione
industriale del lino
rappresentava un
caposaldo
dell'economia per
l'Irlanda del Nord.

On the other side of the Atlantic a group of tailors – probably from the same immigrant family – ply their trade in a New York tenement, 1900. Few worked longer hours than these contract workers.

Al otro lado del Atlántico, un grupo de sastres, probablemente de la misma familia de inmigrantes, en plena tarea en un taller de Nueva York, 1900. Pocos trabajaban tantas horas como estos obreros a destajo.

Dall'altra parte dell'Atlantico, un gruppo di sarti, probabilmente della stessa famiglia di immigrati, esercitano il loro mestiere nella loro casa in affitto a New York, 1900. L'orario di chi lavorava a cottimo era il più lungo di tutti.

Dockers unload barrels from a ship in Portsmouth harbour, on the English south coast, 1900. British dockers were among the most militant in the early 20th century, and among the most poorly paid.

Obreros portuarios descargan barriles de un barco en el puerto de Portsmouth, en la costa sur de Inglaterra, en 1900. A principios del siglo XX, los obreros portuarios británicos eran unos de los más militantes, y también unos de los peor pagados.

Degli scaricatori di porto prelevano dei barili da una nave sul molo di Portsmouth, nella costa meridionale della Gran Bretagna, 1900. Al principio del XX secolo, i lavoratori portuali erano tra i più attivi politicamente e tra i più malpagati.

Lumber is prepared
for use in paper
making, Washington
State, USA, 1900.
It was the state's most
valuable commodity.

Madera destinada a la
fabricación de papel,
estado de Washington,
Estados Unidos, 1900.
Era la materia prima
más codiciada de este
estado.

Preparazione del
legno per l'industria
cartaria, Stato di
Washington, USA,
1900. Era il prodotto
più prezioso di questa
regione.

The interior of a box tower at a petrol works in Prededussport, Romania, 1909. More valuable, more sought-after and of greater use than gold, oil was already beginning to replace coal in the 1900s.

Interior de una torre de extracción en un pozo de petróleo de Prededussport, Rumanía, 1909. Más valioso, útil y buscado que el oro, el crudo empezó a sustituir al carbón a principios del siglo XX.

L'interno di una torre per l'estrazione del petrolio a Prededussport, Romania, 1909. Più prezioso, più ambito e molto più utile dell'oro, in quegli anni il petrolio stava già iniziando a prendere il posto del carbone.

An oilfield at Saratoga, Texas, April 1908. The biggest oil producer in the world was the United States, and the heart of the American oil industry was in Texas.

Un campo de petróleo en Saratoga, Texas, abril de 1908. Estados Unidos era el primer productor mundial de crudo y Texas era el centro de la industria petrolera americana.

Un giacimento petrolifero a Saratoga, Texas, aprile 1908. Il paese con maggior produzione di petrolio al mondo erano gli Stati Uniti, ed il Texas era il cuore dell'industria petrolifera americana.

(Above) The wild days of the American West were over, but there was still plenty of work for ranch hands at the Matador Ranch, Texas, 1908, photographed by Erwin E Smith. (Opposite) Itinerant sheep shearers, Westmoreland, England, 1900.

(Arriba) La época del salvaje oeste americano había terminado, pero aún quedaba mucho trabajo en el rancho Matador, Texas, en 1908. La fotografía es de Erwin E. Smith. (Página siguiente) Esquiladores de ovejas itinerantes, Westmoreland, Inglaterra, 1900.

(In alto) L'epoca selvaggia del far west era ormai terminata, ma c'era ancora moltissimo lavoro per questi cowboy del Matador Ranch, fotografati da Erwin E. Smith, Texas, 1908. (Pagina a fianco) Tosatori di pecore transumanti, Westmoreland, Inghilterra, 1900.

In an age that was only just beginning to flirt with impropriety, there was still employment for this bathing-machine attendant, somewhere on the coast of England, 1900. But a new morality threatened.

En una época que estaba a punto de caer en la indecencia moral, aún había trabajo para esta asistenta de cabinas de baño móviles, en algún lugar de la costa de Inglaterra, en 1900. La nueva "moral" amenazaba con imponerse.

In un'epoca in cui ci si iniziava ad abituare al rilassamento dei costumi, c'era ancora posto per dei mestieri come questo, custode di cabine per il bagno, da qualche parte lungo la costa inglese, 1900. Ma una nuova moralità si affacciava minacciosa.

New Year's Day 1909, and a new Act comes into force: some 500,000 elderly in Britain – including these two – become pensioners for the first time, eligible for weekly payments from the Government.

Día de Año Nuevo de 1909. Entra en vigor una nueva ley en Gran Bretaña: 500.000 personas mayores, incluyendo las de la foto, se convierten en pensionistas por primera vez, con derecho a recibir una pensión semanal del Gobierno.

Capodanno del 1909, entra in vigore una nuova legge: circa 500.000 anziani in Gran Bretagna, compresi questi due, prendono per la prima volta una pensione settimanale assegnata loro dal Governo.

7. Leisure
Ocio
Tempo libero

It was the simplest, happiest and most innocent of pleasures.
A day at the seaside meant donkey rides and ice-creams, walks along
the esplanade, fun at the slot machines, and paddling in the sea.
Two women enjoy the delights of the beach, 1902.

El placer más sencillo, feliz e inocente. Un día de playa: paseos en
burro y por el frente marítimo, helados, emoción en las máquinas
tragaperras y un poco de chapoteo en el mar. En la foto, dos mujeres
disfrutan de los placeres de la playa, 1902.

Era il più semplice, il più allegro e il più innocente dei piaceri.
Durante una giornata al mare si poteva passeggiare a dorso d'asino
o mangiare un gelato, camminare sul lungomare, divertirsi con le slot
machine o sguazzare nell'acqua. Due donne si godono una giornata
in spiaggia, 1902.

7. Leisure
Ocio
Tempo libero

Wages were rising early in the 20th century, and the pioneer work of Thomas Cook and his 'day excursions' a generation earlier was greatly extended by the rapid development of the internal combustion engine. Nowhere was safe from the whirring wheels of the tripper, the tourist, the excursionist. Families and courting couples, historical societies and Sunday schools, young 'blades' in boaters and young 'gels' in fancy hats, all flocked to the countryside, the moors, the woods and, above all, the seaside.

Leisure was an active experience for the Edwardians and their contemporaries. The public baths, the public libraries, many of the pubs and almost all other institutions were closed on Sundays. There remained the great outdoors, and that is where many went.

But the seaside was always the favourite destination. Brighton, Atlantic City, Coney Island, Le Touquet, Deauville, San Sebastian, Nice and Monte-Carlo (for those who could afford it) grew in size and wealth and in the number of joys that they had to offer. There were piers and Pierrots, aquariums and amusement arcades, brass bands and bathing machines, saucy delights and mile after mile of golden sand. For a while at least, the desk, the loom, the coalface and the school desk seemed a lifetime away.

A principios del siglo XX aumentaron los salarios, y los trabajos pioneros de Thomas Cook y sus "excursiones de un día", realizados una generación antes, se difundieron ampliamente gracias al rápido desarrollo del motor de combustión interna. Ya no quedaba ningún lugar a salvo de las ruedas de los viajeros, turistas o excursionistas. Familias enteras, parejas de enamorados, sociedades históricas y escuelas dominicales, chicos con sombreros *canotier* y chicas con sombreros informales, todos acudían en masa al campo, la montaña, el bosque y, sobre todo, la playa.

El ocio se convirtió en una estimulante actividad para los ciudadanos de la sociedad de Eduardo VII. Los baños públicos, las bibliotecas, muchos de los *pubs* y casi todos los demás establecimientos cerraban los domingos, y la gente prefería pasar el día al aire libre.

El destino favorito de la mayoría era la playa. Brighton, Atlantic City, Coney Island, Le Touquet, Deauville, San Sebastián, Niza y Montecarlo (para los que se lo podían permitir) crecieron en tamaño y riqueza y también en oferta turística. Malecones y Pierrots, acuarios y galerías de ocio, bandas de música y cabinas de baño, todo tipo de placeres aguardaban a los visitantes, sin contar, por supuesto, con los kilómetros y kilómetros de arena dorada. Por unos instantes, la oficina, el telar, la mina o la escuela parecían de otro mundo.

Ai primi del secolo, i salari erano in aumento e le "gite di un giorno", lanciate dal pioniere Thomas Cook qualche decennio prima, iniziavano ad avere un grande successo grazie al rapido sviluppo del motore a scoppio. Non c'era posto in cui sentirsi al sicuro dalle ruote sfreccianti di viaggiatori, turisti ed escursionisti. Famiglie e coppiette, società storiche e scuole di catechismo, baldi giovanottoni con i loro cappelli di paglia e giovani donzelle con i loro fantasiosi copricapi, tutti si precipitavano in campagna, in brughiera, nei boschi e soprattutto al mare.

Il tempo libero era pieno di attività movimentate per i contemporanei di Edoardo VII, in Gran Bretagna come nel resto del mondo. I bagni pubblici, le biblioteche, molti pub e quasi tutte le altre istituzioni erano chiuse di domenica. Non restava che la vita all'aperto, e chi poteva non perdeva certo l'occasione.

La spiaggia era il luogo di destinazione più popolare. Brighton, Atlantic City, Coney Island, Le Touquet, Deauville, San Sebastian, Nizza e Montecarlo (per chi se lo poteva permettere) crescevano per dimensioni, ricchezza e numero di attrazioni che avevano da offrire: passeggiate sul lungomare e teatrini, acquari e sale giochi, bande musicali e cabine su ruote per il bagno, viste piccanti e chilometri e chilometri di spiagge dorate. Almeno per un po', ci si dimenticava delle miniere di carbone e dei banchi di scuola.

The pleasures of the seaside were shared by all, young and old, sophisticated and naïve, the mighty and the humble. Here members of the Rothschild family shelter from the winds of fortune, c. 1909.

Los placeres de la playa eran compartidos por todo el mundo, jóvenes y viejos, intelectuales y analfabetos, poderosos y humildes. En la foto, miembros de la familia Rothschild al abrigo de los vientos de la fortuna, hacia 1909.

Tutti potevano godersi una giornata in spiaggia, giovani e anziani, le persone più sofisticate e le più semplici, quelle più potenti e le più umili. Qui, alcuni membri della famiglia Rothschild al riparo dai venti sfavorevoli, ca. 1909.

Bathers still used these monstrous bathing machines to change into their costume for a 'dip in the briny'. And horses still pulled them in and out of the sea for the convenience of the modest. An English resort, c. 1909.

Los bañistas aún usaban estas aparatosas cabinas para cambiarse antes de remojarse en el mar. Con la ayuda de caballos, entraban y salían del agua para comodidad de los más pudorosos. Un balneario inglés, hacia 1909.

I bagnanti utilizzavano ancora queste mostruose cabine da bagno per cambiarsi il costume e "tuffarsi nel blu". Erano trainate da cavalli fino alla linea d'acqua, ideali per le persone pudiche. Una località di villeggiatura inglese, ca. 1909.

The greatest fun of all was to challenge the incoming tide with the
biggest sandcastle anyone had ever made. Alfred Hind Robinson's
lovely panorama of the beach at Bamburgh, Northumberland,
c. 1909, encapsulates the essence of the pleasure.

La mayor diversión era desafiar a la marea entrante con el castillo
de arena más grande jamás construido. Esta bella foto de Alfred
Hind Robinson de la playa de Bamburgh, Northumberland, hacia
1909, capta la esencia de tan singular placer.

Il più grande dei divertimenti era quello di sfidare la marea con
un castello di sabbia dalle dimensioni eccezionali. La splendida
immagine della spiaggia di Bamburgh, nel Northumberland,
ripresa da Alfred Hind Robinson intorno al 1909, riassume
l'essenza di questo piacere.

They came in their hundreds, to stroll along the promenade in their
smartest clothes, with their parasols cocked against the sun – for a
tan was most unfashionable. The seafront at Southsea, Portsmouth,
in 1900.

A centenares acudían a deambular por el paseo marítimo, con sus ropas
más elegantes y los parasoles apuntando al sol, pues el bronceado aún
no estaba de moda. Frente marítimo de Southsea, Portsmouth, 1900.

Giungevano a centinaia, per la passeggiata lungo il corso, nei loro
vestiti più eleganti, con gli ombrellini puntati in cielo per proteggersi
dal sole, la tintarella non era affatto di moda. Il lungomare di Southsea,
Portsmouth, 1900.

In winter there was no better delight than a sing-song around the piano in the parlour. The repertoire was varied – ballads, novelty songs, arias from light opera. One of the most popular of all was *I Do Like To Be Beside The Seaside*. A family gathering around the piano, 1908.

En invierno no había mayor placer que reunirse en un salón para cantar en torno al piano. El repertorio era de lo más variado: baladas, canciones de moda y arias de opereta. Uno de los temas más populares era *I Do Like To Be Beside The Seaside*, literalmente: "Me encanta la playa". En la foto, una familia alrededor de un piano, en 1908.

In inverno, non c'era piacere più grande che riunirsi a cantare qualche canzone attorno al pianoforte, nel salone. Il repertorio era vasto, ballate, canzoni allora di moda e arie di operetta. Una delle più popolari di tutte era *I Do Like To Be Beside The Seaside* (Mi piace davvero stare accanto al mare). Una famiglia attorno al piano, 1908.

Good weather was not essential. A lungful of ozone was as beneficial on
a bracing day as on a fine one. Late Victorian ladies gaze at the splendours
of Eastbourne pier on a cold day in 1900.

No era necesario que hiciera buen tiempo. Un poco de aire fresco era
igualmente tonificante tanto en un día malo como en uno bueno. En la foto,
damas de finales de la era victoriana contemplan la belleza del malecón de
Eastbourne en un frío día de invierno de 1900.

Non era necessario che facesse bel tempo. Una boccata d'aria fresca
faceva bene sia con la pioggia che con il sole. Mentre l'epoca vittoriana
tramontava, alcune donne contemplano lo splendido molo di Eastburne
in una fredda giornata del 1900.

Better than gazing at the pier was to saunter along it. You could weigh yourself, have your fortune told, win a prize, buy a stick of rock, meet the boy or girl of your dreams. Holidaymakers on the Clarence Pier, Southsea, 1900.

Pasear por el malecón era aún más divertido que contemplarlo. Uno podía pesarse, hacerse echar las cartas, ganar un premio, comprar un trozo de roca o encontrar al chico o la chica de sus sueños. En la foto, veraneantes en el paseo del muelle de Clarence, Southsea, 1900.

Una passeggiatina lungo il molo era ancora meglio che stare seduti a guardarlo. Ci si poteva pesare, farsi predire il futuro, vincere un premio, mangiare zucchero filato o incontrare l'uomo o la donna dei sogni. Dei villeggianti sul Clarence Pier, Southsea, 1900.

The notion of animal rights had not yet cramped the style of visitors to the zoo. (Above) Young people enjoy an elephant ride in Regent's Park, London, 1900. (Opposite) A leopard studies an example of the species *Homo sapiens*.

Los derechos de los animales eran aún un concepto extraño para los visitantes del zoo. (Arriba) Unos jóvenes se divierten a lomos de un elefante en Regent's Park, Londres, en 1900. (Página siguiente) Un leopardo estudia el comportamiento de un ejemplar de *Homo sapiens*.

Il concetto dei diritti degli animali ancora non era così diffuso da mettere in soggezione i visitatori dello zoo. (In alto) Dei ragazzi si godono una passeggiata in elefante nel Regent's Park di Londra, 1900. (Pagina a fianco) Un leopardo osserva un esemplare della specie *homo sapiens*.

When it comes to Christmas shopping, little has changed in a hundred years. The notice on the front of this London store begs customers to shop early. They did not then (c. 1909). They do not now.

La época de compras navideñas no ha cambiado mucho en cien años. El cartel de esta tienda londinense anima a los clientes a no dejarlo todo para el último momento. Lo hacían entonces, hacia 1909, y siguen haciéndolo ahora.

Per quel che riguarda le spese natalizie non è cambiato niente rispetto a cento anni fa. Un cartello davanti a questo negozio londinese invita i clienti ad anticipare gli acquisti. Allora nessuno lo faceva (ca. 1909) e adesso neanche.

Crowds gather around the windows of a store in London's Oxford Street, Christmas 1905. It was a good time to be rich enough to buy presents, wait while they were perfectly wrapped, then take them home in a taxi.

La gente se acerca al escaparate de una tienda de Oxford Street, en Londres, en las Navidades de 1905. Si se tenía suficiente dinero, era un buen momento para comprar regalos, hacerlos envolver y tomar un taxi de vuelta a casa.

Una folla di gente si accalca davanti alle vetrine di un negozio di Oxford Street, a Londra, nel Natale del 1905. Era una buona epoca per essere abbastanza ricchi da poter comprare i regali, aspettare che li incartassero elegantemente e portarseli a casa in taxi.

For many, the great outdoors beckoned. On Sunday (the only
day free from work) you could cycle in a group to the countryside,
or hire a charabanc to take you. And then, there were all the joys
of a picnic.

Muchos preferían divertirse al aire libre. El domingo, que era el único
día festivo, se hacían excursiones al campo en bicicleta o en "minibús"
y uno se disponía a disfrutar de los encantos del *picnic*.

Erano in molti a sentire il richiamo dell'aria aperta. La domenica (unico
giorno festivo) si poteva andare in campagna con un gruppo di amici in
bicicletta, o affittando la allora popolarissima giardiniera. E una volta
arrivati, ci si godeva un bel picnic.

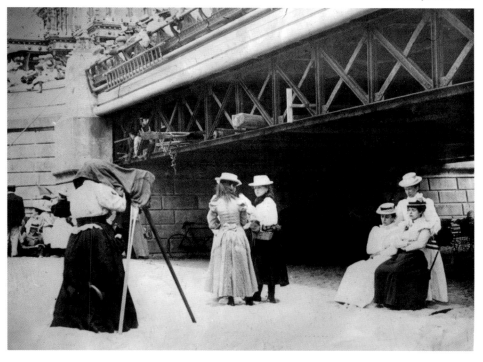

A woman photographer at work on Southend beach, June 1905. For Londoners, the two most popular seaside destinations were Brighton and Southend. Brighton was bigger and brasher, but Southend had the world's longest pier.

Una fotógrafa en pleno trabajo en la playa de Southend, en junio de 1905. Para los londinenses, los dos destinos costeros más populares eran Brighton y Southend. Brighton era más concurrido y animado, pero Southend tenía el malecón más grande del mundo.

Una fotografa in azione presso la spiaggia di Southend, nel giugno del 1905. Le località balneari più ambite dai londinesi erano Brighton e Southend. Brighton era più grande e più movimentata, ma Southend aveva il molo più lungo del mondo.

For the more adventurous, there were the joys and perils of mountaineering. Clothes were hardly designed for the rigours of the descent into a crevasse on the Mer de Glace, but they may well have softened the landing in the event of a fall.

Los más aventureros preferían la emoción y los peligros de la montaña, y, aunque la ropa no fuera adecuada a las dificultades que suponía descender por una roca en Mer de Glace, podía amortiguar el golpe en caso de sufrir una caída.

I più temerari affrontavano i pericoli e la bellezza della montagna. Gli indumenti non erano certo appropriati per una discesa nei crepacci ghiacciati del Mer de Glace, ma di certo potevano attutire l'impatto in caso di caduta.

Rock climbing was for the truly athletic – and for those who could never imagine a rope fraying on a rock edge.

La escalada estaba reservada a los más atléticos, y a los que nunca hubieran imaginado que una cresta rocosa pudiera romper una cuerda.

Le scalate erano riservate ai fisici più atletici – e a chi non avrebbe mai potuto immaginare che una corda potesse spezzarsi sfregandosi contro una roccia.

Members of the Salvation Army farm colony at Hadleigh, Suffolk, prepare
for the start of a piggy-back race, December 1905. The 'Sally Army' was by
then just over 25 years old and had already done much to relieve poverty.

Miembros de la colonia agrícola del Ejército de Salvación en Hadleigh, Suffolk,
se preparan para una carrera a cuestas, diciembre de 1905. Este "ejército" tenía
entonces más de 25 años de antigüedad y había luchado mucho contra la
pobreza.

Alcuni membri della comunità agricola dell'Esercito della Salvezza ad Hadleigh,
nel Suffolk, pronti allo scatto per una corsa a cavalluccio, dicembre 1905. Il
"Sally Army" aveva appena compiuto 25 anni ed aveva già fatto molto per
alleviare le sofferenze dei più poveri.

Early days of health and beauty. A group of women perform gymnastic exercises in the yard of what may well be a training college, 1905. Swedish drill was extremely popular in the 1900s.

Comienzos del culto a la belleza y la salud. Un grupo de mujeres realiza ejercicios gimnásticos en el patio de lo que podría ser un colegio, 1905. La gimnasia sueca era muy popular a principios del siglo XX.

Primi vagiti per il culto a un corpo sano e bello. Un gruppo di donne esegue esercizi di ginnastica nel cortile di un edificio che potrebbe essere un istituto magistrale, 1905. La ginnastica svedese andava molto di moda ai primi del Novecento.

A series of hard
winters in Europe
led to a considerable
increase in the
popularity of
skating. Young
men take to the
ice on a frozen
lake at Courbit
Walsh, Spalding,
Lincolnshire, in
January 1908.

Gracias a una serie
de fríos inviernos
en Europa, el
patinaje sobre
hielo se convirtió
en un deporte muy
popular. En la foto,
unos jóvenes patinan
sobre un lago helado
en Courbit Walsh,
Spalding,
Lincolnshire,
enero de 1908.

Il pattinaggio sul
ghiaccio assunse una
popolarità enorme,
grazie anche al
succedersi di inverni
freddissimi in tutta
Europa. Alcuni
giovanotti si
lanciano sulla
superficie ghiacciata
di un lago presso
Courbit Walsh,
Spalding, nel
Lincolnshire,
gennaio 1908.

Gentle decline... A young woman takes part in an impromptu programme of winter sports at Buxton in the English Peak District, 1904. Her hatpin seems to be withstanding the test.

Un suave descenso... Una joven participa en una competición espontánea de deportes de invierno en Buxton, en el distrito inglés de Peak, en 1904. De momento, su sombrero parece superar la prueba.

Dolce pendio... Una ragazza prende parte ad un programma impromptu di sport invernali a Buxton, nel distretto di English Peak, 1904. Pare che lo spillone del suo cappello sia in grado di superare la prova.

Fast descent… Spectators rise to their feet as an Englishwoman hurtles past on the Cresta Run at St Moritz, Switzerland, 1908. Many women wanted considerably more than the vote.

Un rápido descenso… Los espectadores saltan al ver cómo esta inglesa se lanza a toda velocidad durante la carrera de Cresta, Saint Moritz, Suiza, 1908. No todas las mujeres se conformaban con el derecho al voto.

Discesa rapida… Alcuni spettatori si alzano in piedi mentre una ragazza inglese sfreccia pericolosamente lungo la storica Cresta Run di St. Moritz, Svizzera, 1908. Chiaro che molte donne non si accontentavano solo del diritto al voto.

Hot air balloons
prepare for take-off
from the grounds
of the fashionable
Hurlingham Club,
London, in May
1909.

Globos aerostáticos
se disponen a
levantar el vuelo
desde el elitista
club Hurlingham,
Londres, mayo de
1909.

Mongolfiere pronte
al decollo sulla pista
dell'Hurlingham
Club, uno dei
club più in voga
di Londra,
maggio 1909.

In an age when all true Englishmen believed that Britannia still ruled the waves, the height of the London Season was the Cowes Regatta, held annually off the coast of the Isle of Wight. Britannia was to be severely tested a few years later.

En una época en que ningún inglés dudaba del dominio de Gran Bretaña sobre todos los mares del planeta, asistimos al momento culminante de la temporada veraniega londinense, la regata de Cowes, que se celebraba anualmente en las costas de la Isla de Wight. Uno años más tarde, la flota británica recibiría un duro revés.

In un'epoca in cui ogni inglese vero era convinto che la Gran Bretagna ancora governasse i mari, il momento culminante della stagione londinese era la Cowes Regatta, una regata che si teneva ogni anno al largo dell'Isola di Wight. L'impero britannico sarà messo duramente alla prova qualche anno più tardi.

8. Entertainment
Espectáculos
Spettacolo

Mathieson Lang as Philippe Marchiali in the 1909 production
The Prisoner of the Bastille. From its very beginnings, the 'picture palace'
swept all before it. Huge audiences flocked to every converted theatre,
hall, pavilion or purpose-built cinema.

Mathieson Lang interpreta el papel de Philippe Marchiali en la producción
inglesa de *El prisionero de la Bastilla* (1909). Desde el principio, el cine
provocó un cambio radical de escenario, y el público acudió en masa a
los teatros, salones o pabellones reconvertidos y a las salas de cine de
nueva construcción.

Mathieson Lang interpreta Philippe Marchiali nella produzione del 1909
Il prigioniero della Bastiglia. Sin dai suoi inizi, il cinematografo spazza via
tutti i suoi antecessori. Un numero incredibile di spettatori accorre nei
teatri, nei saloni e nei padiglioni trasformati in cinema o nelle sale
costruite ad hoc.

8. Entertainment
Espectáculos
Spettacolo

By the mid-1900s 'biographs', 'kinemas' and 'picture palaces' had opened in most towns of any size in Europe and the United States. They were popular and successful beyond the wildest dreams of Georges Méliès – whose dreams tended to be on the wild side. From this time the days of the music-hall and the vaudeville theatre were numbered, though both had many more years of popularity and hilarity ahead of them.

A new invention called the gramophone was beginning to bring the voices and the artistry of the world's top singers and comedians into the parlours of the middle classes. Unlike the cinema, it posed no threat to live performances. More people stepped out onto the dance floors of hotels and assembly rooms, parochial halls and country clubs than ever before. Daringly they danced the tango and the waltz, slipping breathlessly back into their seats for a cup of tea or a refreshing cordial.

As for the entertainers, they no longer performed for predominantly local audiences. Their fame travelled swiftly before them, and they were booked to appear in other cities, states, countries and even other continents. The age of the international star was under way.

A mediados de la década de 1900, la mayoría de las ciudades de Europa y Estados Unidos ya contaban con salas de cine, que tuvieron un éxito y una aceptación muy superiores a lo que Georges Méliès hubiera llegado a imaginar, y eso que imaginación no le faltaba precisamente. Desde entonces, la época del *music-hall* y el vodevil tenía los días contados, aunque a estos antiguos espectáculos todavía les quedaban años de gran popularidad.

Un nuevo invento, denominado gramófono, introdujo en los salones de la clase media las voces y el arte de los mejores cantantes y comediantes del mundo. A diferencia del cine, el gramófono no suponía ninguna amenaza para las actuaciones en directo. Todo lo contrario. La gente acudía más que nunca a las salas de baile de hoteles, parroquias y clubs campestres. Tras una buena sesión de tangos y valses, era obligado volver a los asientos para recuperar el aliento y tomar una taza de té o un refresco.

Los artistas dejaron de actuar principalmente para un público local, como ocurría hasta entonces, y su fama les precedía por dondequiera que viajasen. Actuaban en otras ciudades, en otros países e incluso en otros continentes. Los tiempos de las grandes estrellas internacionales no estaban ya muy lejos.

Verso la metà del decennio, i cosiddetti "cinemà", chiamati poi "cinematografi Lumière" e infine cinema o cine, avevano aperto in quasi tutte le città, grandi e piccole, in Europa e negli Stati Uniti. La loro popolarità ed il loro successo andava ben oltre le più rosee aspettative di Georges Méliès, che era tra l'altro un personaggio assai ottimista. Gli spettacoli musicali e di varietà avevano i giorni contati, malgrado entrambi fossero colonne storiche della comicità popolare.

Una nuova invenzione denominata grammofono portava, nei saloni della media borghesia, la voce ed il virtuosismo dei migliori cantanti e comici del mondo. Al contrario del cinema, ciò non rappresentava una minaccia per le esibizioni dal vivo. Erano sempre di più le persone che si lanciavano a ballare nelle piste degli hotel, nei saloni da ballo, nelle sale parrocchiali e nei circoli ricreativi, al ritmo del tango o del valzer, per poi rifugiarsi di nuovo, senza respiro, nelle loro poltrone a bere una tazza di tè o un cordiale ristoratore.

Dal canto loro, gli artisti non si esibivano più per una ristretta cerchia di spettatori. La loro fama li precedeva sempre e venivano chiamati in altre città, regioni, stati e perfino in altri continenti. Stava iniziando l'epoca delle star internazionali.

Dance of death.
Margarete Geertruida
Zelle, better known as
Mata Hari, performs
her notorious
'Dance of the Seven
Veils', 1907.

La danza de la muerte.
Margarete Geertruida
Zelle, más conocida
como Mata Hari,
interpreta su célebre
danza de los siete
velos, 1907.

La danza della morte.
Margarete Geertruida
Zelle, più nota come
Mata Hari, si esibisce
nella sua famigerata
"Danza dei sette veli",
1907.

Her coquetry may well have contributed to her conviction as a spy and her execution by firing squad during the First World War.

Se dice que su coquetería contribuyó a que fuera condenada por espía y ejecutada por un pelotón de fusilamiento durante la Primera Guerra Mundial.

La sua civetteria fu senza dubbio una delle cause per cui fu accusata di spionaggio e fucilata da un plotone di esecuzione durante la Prima guerra mondiale.

Early cinematic violence – French-style. The execution scene from a Georges Méliès film, *L'histoire d'un crime*, made in 1906. So violent was the scene considered that it was suppressed by the police.

Primeras escenas de violencia en el cine al estilo francés. En *La historia de un crimen*, de Georges Méliès, rodada en 1906, la escena de la ejecución fue considerada tan violenta que la policía la censuró.

Prime immagini di violenza sugli schermi, "alla francese". La scena dell'esecuzione da un film di George Méliès, *L'histoire d'un crime*, girata nel 1906. Fu subito considerata eccessivamente violenta e censurata dalle autorità.

Early cinematic violence – American-style. The murder scene from Edwin S Potter's *The Great Train Robbery*, 1903. Despite crude sets and acting, its action and narrative pace made it a huge success.

Primeras escenas de violencia en el cine al estilo americano. Un asesinato en la película *The great train robbery* (1903), de Edwin S. Potter. A pesar de tener unos escenarios rudimentarios y una pobre interpretación, la acción y el ritmo narrativo la convirtieron en un gran éxito.

Prime immagini di violenza sugli schermi, "all'americana". La scena dell'omicidio da *L'assalto al treno postale* di Edwin S. Porter, 1903. Malgrado l'ingenuità della scenografia e della recitazione, l'azione e il ritmo narrativo gli procurarono un enorme successo.

(Opposite) Ehrich Weiss, the rabbi's son who became Harry Houdini, 1900. Houdini was the greatest magician and escapologist of his age. (Above) Signor Martino uses his powers to levitate Mlle Nita on stage, 1900.

(Página anterior) Ehrich Weiss, el hijo del rabino que se convirtió en Harry Houdini, en 1900. Houdini fue el mago y escapista más grande de su época. (Arriba) Signor Martino usa sus poderes para hacer levitar a la señorita Nita sobre el escenario, 1900.

(Pagina a fianco) Erhich Weiss, il figlio di un rabbino che si trasformò nel Grande Houdini, 1900. Harry Houdini era il più grande mago e prestigiatore dell'epoca. (In alto) Il Signor Martino fa uso dei suoi poteri per far levitare Madamoiselle Nita sul palcoscenico, 1900.

An early jazz band, 1900. The costumes are similar to those worn by bands that led mourners through the streets of New Orleans during a funeral. A saxophone quintet, however, was something of a novelty.

Una de las primeras bandas de *jazz*, en 1900. Sus trajes son similares a los de las orquestas que acompañaban a los cortejos fúnebres por las calles de Nueva Orleans, pero un quinteto de saxofonistas era ciertamente toda una novedad.

Una delle prime bande di jazz, 1900. Gli indumenti sono simili a quelli usati dalle orchestre che accompagnavano i funerali nelle strade di New Orleans. Un quintetto di sassofoni, tuttavia, era una grande novità.

The classic 'cakewalk', photographed in Paris on 13 December 1903. Some black performers already preferred European audiences.

El clásico baile *cakewalk*, en una foto tomada en París el 13 de diciembre de 1903. En esa época, algunos artistas de color ya preferían el público europeo.

Il classico passo di danza "cakewalk", fotografato a Parigi il 13 dicembre del 1903. Alcuni artisti di colore iniziavano a preferire il pubblico europeo.

(Opposite) The last performance at the Lambeth music-hall, south London, 1900. (Right) Dan Leno as the Dame in *Jack and the Beanstalk* at the Drury Lane Theatre.

(Página anterior) La última representación en el *music-hall* Lambeth, al sur de Londres, en 1900. (Derecha) Dan Leno interpreta a la madre del protagonista en *Jack and the Beanstalk*, en el teatro Drury Lane.

(Pagina a fianco) L'ultimo spettacolo al teatro di varietà Lambeth, al sud di Londra, 1900. (A destra) Dan Leno interpreta la madre del piccolo eroe in *Jack e la pianta di fagioli* al teatro Drury Lane.

A risqué and ill-contrived tableau of devils and innocents at Le Cirque music-hall, Paris, 1900. It was an immense success.

Un arriesgado y lúgubre cuadro vivo de demonios e inocentes en el *music-hall* Le Cirque, París, 1900. Tuvo un éxito enorme.

Un'interpretazione rischiosa e avventata di diavoli e innocenti al teatro di varietà Le Cirque, Parigi, 1900. Ebbe un successo grandioso.

Sex and splendour
at the Folies-Bergère,
1909. The costume
was heavy, and to
dance in it would
have courted disaster.

Sexo y esplendor en
el Folies-Bergère,
1909. Este vestido
era tan pesado que
intentar bailar con él
habría sido incluso
peligroso.

Sesso e splendore alle
Folies-Bergère, 1909.
Con quel pesante
costume, poteva
finire male se si
provava a ballare.

Easter surprise.
Actresses, musical
comedy stars and
sisters Phyllis and
Zena Dare pose with
a giant egg, 1905.

Sorpresa de Pascua.
Las hermanas Phyllis
y Zena Dare,
actrices y *vedettes* de
comedias musicales,
posan con un huevo
gigante, 1905.

Sorpresa di Pasqua.
Le sorelle Phyllis
e Zena Dare,
attrici e star delle
commedie musicali,
posano con un uovo
gigante, 1905.

Eastern delight. A scene from the comic opera *See-See* by Charles Brookfield and Sidney Jones. Following the success of *The Mikado* and *Chu Chin Chow*, the Orient was much in vogue as a setting for stage musicals.

Delicia de Pascua. Escena de la ópera cómica *See-See* de Charles Brookfield y Sidney Jones. Después del éxito de *El Mikado* y *Chu Chin Chow*, Oriente se puso de moda en los teatros musicales de la época.

Delizie di Pasqua. Una scena dall'opera comica *See-See* di Charles Brookfield e Sidney Jones. Dopo il successo di *The Mikado e Chu Chin Chow*, l'Oriente era un'ambientazione molto di moda per le commedie musicali.

French cheek…
A young Maurice
Chevalier on a
promotional
postcard advertising
his appearance at
the Casino Fontaine,
c. 1909.

Desparpajo
francés… Un joven
Maurice Chevalier
en una tarjeta
promocional
que anuncia su
actuación en el
casino Fontaine,
hacia 1909.

Sfrontatezza
francese…
Un giovanissimo
Maurice Chevalier
in una cartolina
postale per far
pubblicità al suo
spettacolo al Casino
Fontaine, ca. 1909.

French chic… The singer, dancer and actress Jeanne Marie Bourgeois, known to her adoring audiences as Mistinguett, c. 1900.

Glamour francés… La cantante, bailarina y actriz Jeanne Marie Bourgeois, más conocida como Mistinguett por su público, hacia 1900.

Raffinatezza francese… La cantante, attrice e ballerina Jeanne Marie Bourgeois, più nota ai suoi devoti ammiratori come Mistinguett, ca. 1900.

Heroes of
the Wild West.
(Opposite) 'Buffalo
Bill' (William
Frederick Cody),
c. 1900. (Right)
Annie Oakley
(Phoebe Anne
Oakley Moses).

Héroes del salvaje
oeste. (Página
anterior) *Buffalo* Bill
(William Frederick
Cody), hacia 1900.
(Derecha) Annie
Oakley (Phoebe
Anne Oakley Moses).

Eroi del far west.
(Pagina a fianco)
"Buffalo Bill"
(William Frederick
Cody), ca. 1900.
(A destra) Annie
Oakley (Phoebe
Anne Oakley Moses).

(Above) The stars of Phineas T Barnum's freak show, c. 1905. From left: Laloo (two bodies), Young Herman (vast chest), J K Coffey (human skeleton), James Morris (rubber face) and Jo Jo (dog face). (Opposite) A close-up of Jo Jo.

(Arriba) Las estrellas del espectáculo de monstruos de Phineas T. Barnum, hacia 1905. De izquierda a derecha: Laloo (dos cuerpos), Young Herman (pecho enorme), J. K. Coffey (esqueleto humano), James Morris (cara de goma) y Jo Jo (cara de perro). (Página anterior) Un primer plano de Jo Jo.

(In alto) Le star dello spettacolo di mostri di Phineas T. Barnum, ca. 1905. Da sinistra: Laloo (due corpi), Young Herman (petto enorme), J. K. Coffey (scheletro umano), James Morris (faccia di gomma) e Jo Jo (faccia di cane). (Pagina a fianco) Un primo piano di Jo Jo.

The genius of Georges Méliès was that he combined popular elements of stage magic with the technological opportunities created by the moving picture. (Above and opposite) Méliès' great metamorphosis.

El genio de Georges Méliès consistió en combinar elementos populares de la magia en vivo con las posibilidades tecnológicas creadas por el cinematógrafo. (Arriba y página siguiente) La gran metamorfosis de Méliès.

La genialità di Georges Méliès consisteva nell'applicare agli elementi degli spettacoli di magia allora in voga, tutte le possibilità tecnologiche che offriva la cinematografia. (In alto e nella pagina a fianco) La grande metamorfosi di Méliès.

It was a simple enough trick to turn a sleeping woman into a butterfly – though getting the butterfly into the air may have been a little tricky – but audiences loved it, and Méliès made a fortune.

Convertir una mujer dormida en una mariposa era un truco bastante sencillo (hacerla volar ya era un poco más difícil), pero al público le encantaba y Méliès hizo fortuna con este truco.

Era un trucco abbastanza semplice, quello di trasformare in farfalla una donna addormentata – anche se poi, farla volare sarebbe risultato un po' più complicato – ma il pubblico lo adorava e Méliès fece fortuna.

9. The Arts
Las artes
Arte

The brilliant dancer Adolphe Bolm of the Russian Imperial Ballet Company in the title role of the ballet *Prince Igor*, 1909. At this time Bolm was accompanying Anna Pavlova on her first tours.

El gran bailarín Adolphe Bolm, de la compañía imperial de *ballet* rusa, en el papel principal de *El príncipe Igor*, en 1909. En esta época, Bolm acompañaba a Anna Pavlova en sus primeras giras.

Il brillante ballerino Adolphe Bolm della compagnia del Balletto Imperiale Russo nel ruolo principale dell'opera *Il principe Igor*, 1909. In quell'epoca, Bolm accompagnava Anna Pavlova nelle sue prime tournée.

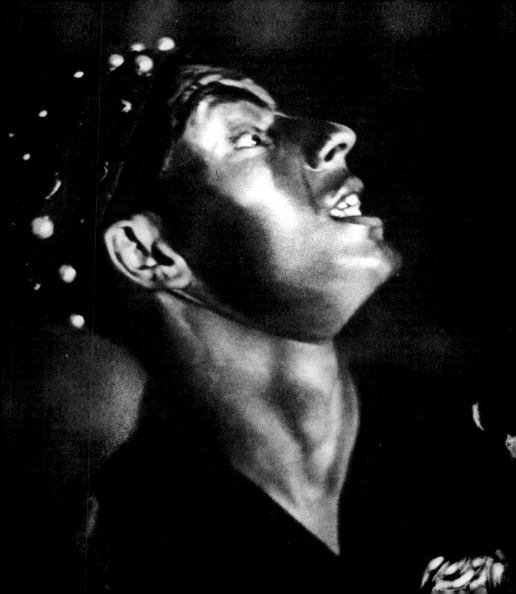

9. The Arts
Las artes
Arte

Artistically, the 1900s may lay claim to being the most exciting decade the world has ever known. An astonishing array of creative genius poured forth plays and novels, symphonies and scores, poems, sculptures and ideas that transformed the way people viewed the world they lived in. It was the age of Shaw and Strindberg, Braque and Picasso, art nouveau and Auguste Rodin, Schönberg and Mahler, Ravel and de Falla, Elgar and Rachmaninov, E M Forster and H G Wells, the last works of Zola and the first works of Thomas Mann.

The decade began with Freud's *The Interpretation of Dreams* and the first performances of Puccini's *Tosca* and *Madame Butterfly*. It ended with the dancers of Diaghilev's Ballets Russes blazing their way across the stage of the Châtelet in Paris. In 1901 the teenage Picasso set up his studio in Montmartre and painted *The Blue Room*, and the Moscow Art Theatre under Stanislavsky gave the first performance of Chekhov's *Three Sisters*. Every year had its clutch of masterworks, and the audiences flocked to see them.

And then there were the performers, the interpreters... Caruso, Pavlova, Nijinsky, Paderewski, Cortot, Ysaÿe, the young Galli-Curci and the more mature Nellie Melba... Across the Atlantic, Joe 'King' Oliver was beginning to warm up his cornet.

Desde el punto de vista artístico, la década de 1900 puede presumir de ser la más creativa de la historia. Una impresionante retahíla de genios produjo extraordinarias novelas y obras de teatro, sinfonías y partituras, poemas, esculturas e ideas que transformaron la manera en que la gente entendía el mundo. Fue la época de Shaw y Strindberg, Braque y Picasso, el *art nouveau* y Auguste Rodin, Schönberg y Mahler, Ravel y Manuel de Falla, Elgar y Rachmaninov, E. M. Forster y H. G. Wells, las últimas obras de Zola y las primeras de Thomas Mann.

La década se inauguró con *La interpretación de los sueños* de Freud y con las primeras representaciones de *Tosca y Madame Butterfly*, de Puccini, y terminó con los bailarines de los *ballets* rusos de Diaghilev cruzando con sus piruetas el escenario de Châtelet, en París. En 1901, un jovencísimo Picasso abrió su estudio en Montmartre y pintó *Habitación azul*, y la compañía Art Theatre de Moscú, bajo la dirección de Stanislavsky, llevó a cabo el primer montaje de *Las tres hermanas* de Chekhov. Cada año tuvo sus obras maestras y el público acudía entusiasmado a disfrutarlas.

También hubo excelentes músicos e intérpretes, como Caruso, Pavlova, Nijinsky, Paderewski, Cortot, Ysaÿe, el joven Galli-Curci y el ya reconocido Nellie Melba, etc. Al otro lado del Atlántico, Joe *King* Oliver empezaba a afinar su corneta...

In quanto alle arti, il primo decennio del secolo è sicuramente il più interessante che il mondo abbia mai conosciuto. Una fitta schiera di geni creativi sfornava commedie e romanzi a non finire, sinfonie e spartiti, poemi, sculture e idee che trasformavano l'immagine che la gente aveva del mondo in cui viveva. Era l'epoca di Shaw e Strindberg, Braque e Picasso, dell'art nouveau e di Auguste Rodin, Schönberg e Mahler, Ravel e De Falla, Elgar e Rachmaninov, E. M. Foster e H. G. Wells, delle ultime opere di Zola e delle prime di Thomas Mann.

Il primo decennio del secolo iniziava con la pubblicazione de *L'interpretazione dei sogni* di Freud e le prime rappresentazioni della *Tosca* e della *Madame butterfly* di Puccini. Terminava con i ballerini dei Ballets Russes di Diaghilev aprendosi strada verso il palco dello Châtelet di Parigi. Nel 1901, un giovanissimo Picasso stabiliva il suo studio a Montmartre e dipingeva la *Stanza blu*, e Stanislavskij si esibiva per la prima volta con *Le tre sorelle* di Čechov. Ogni anno si assisteva alla nascita di nuovi capolavori e la gente accorreva a contemplarli.

E poi c'erano gli attori, gli interpreti... Caruso, Pavlova, Nijinsky, Paderewski, Cortot, Ysaÿe, la giovane Galli-Curci e la più matura Nellie Melba... Dall'altra parte dell'Atlantico, Joe "King" Oliver stava mettendo a punto la sua cornetta.

The *corps de ballet*
of the New York
Metropolitan Opera
house take a break
in their Broadway
rehearsal rooms,
September 1900.

El cuerpo de ballet de
la Metropolitan Opera
de Nueva York se toma
un descanso en las salas
de ensayo de Broadway,
septiembre de 1900.

Il corpo di ballo della
Metropolitan Opera
House di New York
durante una pausa nella
sala prove di Broadway,
settembre 1900.

Tamara Karsavina
in costume for
Michel Fokine's
ballet *Le Pavillon
d'Armide*, 1909.
This was the year she
joined Diaghilev's
Ballets Russes.

Tamara Karsavina
vestida para el *ballet
Le Pavillon d'Armide*,
de Michel Fokine, en
1909, el año en que
se unió a los *ballets*
rusos de Diaghilev.

Tamara Karsavina
in costume per il
balletto *Le Pavillon
d'Armide*, di Michel
Fokine, 1909.
Proprio in quell'anno
si unirà ai Ballets
Russes di Diaghilev.

Anna Pavlova and
Mikhail Mordkin,
c. 1900. Mordkin
had just become
first soloist with the
Bolshoi Company.
Pavlova was barely
16 years old.

Anna Pavlova y
Mijaíl Mordkin,
hacia 1900.
Mordkin acababa
de convertirse en
el primer bailarín
del *ballet* Bolshoi.
Pavlova apenas
tenía 16 años.

Anna Pavlova e
Mikhail Mordkin,
ca. 1900. Mordkin
era appena
diventato primo
ballerino delBolšoj
di Mosca. La
Pavlova era
appena sedicenne.

(Above) Towards the end of his career, the American writer Mark Twain relaxes over a game of billiards, c. 1900. (Opposite) The Irish poet W B Yeats, at the height of his poetic powers, January 1908.

(Arriba) Hacia el final de su carrera, el escritor norteamericano Mark Twain se relaja jugando una partida de billar, hacia 1900. (Página siguiente) El poeta irlandés W. B. Yeats en su época más creativa, enero de 1908.

(In alto) Verso la fine della sua carriera, lo scrittore americano Mark Twain si rilassa giocando al biliardo, ca. 1900. (Pagina a fianco) Il poeta irlandese W. B. Yeats, all'apogeo della sua ispirazione poetica, gennaio 1908.

The Italian tenor Enrico Caruso, photographed just before his first visits to London and New York in 1902 and 1903 respectively.

El tenor italiano Enrico Caruso, fotografiado justo antes de sus primeras visitas a Londres y Nueva York, en 1902 y 1903, respectivamente.

Il tenore italiano Enrico Caruso, fotografato in procinto di partire per la sua prima visita a Londra e a New York, nel 1902 e nel 1903 rispettivamente.

The Australian
soprano Nellie
Melba in the role
of Marguerite in
Faust, c. 1900. She
had yet to inspire
the pudding, sauce
or toast named
after her.

La soprano
australiana Nellie
Melba en el papel
de Margarita, en
una representación
de *Fausto*, hacia
1900, cuando aún
no había inspirado
el postre y la salsa
que llevan su
nombre.

La soprano
australiana Nellie
Melba nel ruolo
di Margherita nel
Faust, ca. 1900.
Più tardi, avrebbe
ispirato il nome
della salsa, delle
pesche e del toast
che portano il suo
nome.

Count Leo Nikolàyevich Tolstoy and his wife Sonya, c. 1905. He lived his last years as a peasant, having denounced wealth and religion as well as his own works.

El conde Leon Tolstoi y su esposa Sonia, hacia 1905. Tolstoi vivió sus últimos años como campesino, tras renunciar al dinero y a la religión, e incluso a su propia obra.

Il conte Lev Nikolàevič Tolstoj e sua moglie Sonia, ca. 1905. Negli ultimi anni della sua vita, Tolstoj si allontanò dalla vita mondana, rifiutando la ricchezza, la religione e perfino le proprie opere.

The novelist and playwright Maxim Gorky (centre, white beard) with the cast of *Smug Citizens*, 1902. It was the year he wrote his greatest play, *The Lower Depths*. He was increasingly involved in the revolutionary movement.

El novelista y dramaturgo Máximo Gorki (en el centro, con barba) con los intérpretes de *Los vagabundos*, en 1902. En ese año escribió su mejor obra de teatro, *Los bajos fondos*. Posteriormente, se implicaría cada vez más en el movimiento revolucionario.

Il romanziere e drammaturgo Maxim Gorky (al centro con la barba bianca) con il cast di *Una famiglia rispettabile*, 1902. Era l'anno in cui scrisse il suo capolavoro, *I bassifondi*. Era sempre più coinvolto nel movimento rivoluzionario.

A study of the
Austrian composer
Gustav Mahler,
c. 1907, the year
he resigned as
conductor of the
Vienna State Opera.

Retrato del
compositor austríaco
Gustav Mahler, hacia
1907, año en que
dimitió como
director de la Ópera
Nacional de Viena.

Un'insolita fotografia
del compositore
austriaco Gustav
Mahler, ca. 1907,
anno in cui
abbandonò il suo
posto di direttore
artistico dell'Opera
imperiale di Vienna.

The French composer Claude Debussy, c. 1909. By this time, he was devoting his talents almost entirely to chamber and piano music.

El compositor francés Claude Debussy, hacia 1909. En esa época se consagró casi totalmente a la música de cámara y para piano.

Il compositore francese Claude Debussy, ca. 1909. In quel periodo, dedicava il suo talento quasi interamente alla musica da camera e al piano.

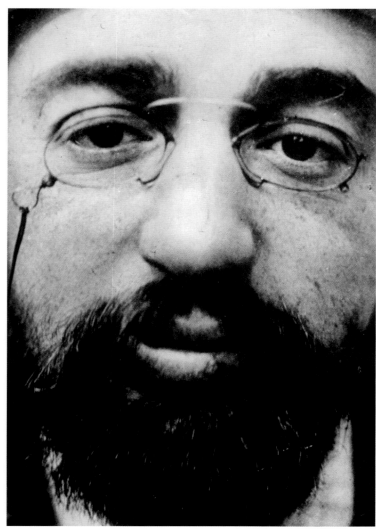

The French painter
Henri de Toulouse-
Lautrec in 1900.
His alcoholism had
induced a complete
breakdown, and
he had only a
year to live.

El pintor francés
Henri de Toulouse-
Lautrec en 1900.
Su alcoholismo le
había hundido
completamente,
y solo le quedaba
un año de vida.

Il pittore francese
Henri de Toulouse-
Lautrec nel 1900.
L'alcolismo lo
stava distruggendo
completamente e
gli rimaneva solo
un anno di vita.

There was, however, still plenty of life left in Pierre-Auguste Renoir, though his hands were becoming crippled with arthritis. He is seen here with friends at his house in Les Collettes, Cagnes, in 1905.

Por el contrario, Pierre-Auguste Renoir estaba aún lleno de vida, a pesar de que sus manos comenzaban a paralizarse debido a la artritis. En la foto, con unos amigos en su casa de Les Collettes, en Cagnes, en 1905.

Al contrario, Pierre-Auguste Renoir era ancora pieno di vita, sebbene le sue mani cominciassero ad intorpidirsi a causa dell'artrite. Qui appare in compagnia di alcuni amici nella sua villa Les Collettes a Cagnes, 1905.

Three of Eadweard Muybridge's magnificent pictures of the American dancer Isadora Duncan, c. 1900. Just as Muybridge revolutionised action photography, so Duncan revolutionised dance.

Tres de las magníficas fotos de la bailarina norteamericana Isadora Duncan realizadas por Eadweard Muybridge, hacia 1900. Si Muybridge revolucionó la fotografía en movimiento, Duncan hizo lo propio con el baile.

Tre magnifiche immagini della ba Isadora Duncan scattate da Eadw Muybridge, ca. 1900. Quest'ultir rivoluzionò il modo di fotografar movimento, e la Duncan trasforr il mondo della danza.

The boy who never grew up – and his creator. (Opposite) Stephanie Stephens as Peter Pan in a 1906 production of J M Barrie's most famous play. (Right) Barrie with Miss A N Emery.

El niño que nunca creció, y su creador. (Página anterior) Stephanie Stephens en el papel de Peter Pan, en una producción de 1906 de la célebre obra de J. M. Barrie. (Derecha) Barrie con A. N. Emery.

Il bambino che non voleva crescere… e il suo creatore. (Pagina a fianco) Stephanie Stephens interpreta Peter Pan in una realizzazione della commedia più famosa di J. M. Barrie. (A destra) Barrie con Miss A. N. Emery.

(Above) The French sculptor Auguste Rodin in his museum at Meudon, c. 1909.
(Opposite) Youth pays light-hearted homage to Edgar Degas (seated, centre),
c. 1900. Almost blind, the great man could barely see the camera.

(Arriba) El escultor francés Auguste Rodin en su museo de Meudon, hacia 1909.
(Página siguiente) La juventud rinde un divertido homenaje a Edgar Degas (sentado,
en el centro), hacia 1900. Casi ciego, el pintor apenas podía ver la cámara.

(In alto) Lo scultore francese Auguste Rodin nel suo museo di Meudon, ca. 1909.
(Pagina a fianco) La gioventù rende un devoto omaggio a Edgar Degas (seduto al
centro), ca. 1900. Ormai quasi cieco, il grande artista poteva a malapena
distinguere la macchina fotografica.

The principal speaker at this protest meeting against a visit to London by Tsar Nicholas in 1908 was George Bernard Shaw (centre, without hat). It was Shaw's proud boast that he was an 'immoralist and heretic'.

El portavoz de esta reunión de protesta contra la visita del zar Nicolás a Londres en 1908 es George Bernard Shaw (en el centro, sin sombrero), que se jactaba de ser "un inmoralista y un hereje".

L'oratore principale, durante questa manifestazione di protesta per la visita a Londra dello zar Nicola II nel 1908, era George Bernard Shaw (al centro, senza il cappello). Lo scrittore si vantava di essere "lassista ed eretico".

Adeline Virginia Stephen (Virginia Woolf) with her father, Sir Leslie Stephen, in 1902. Two years later, her father died and she moved to Bloomsbury where she took up writing. The rest is a stream of consciousness.

Adeline Virginia Stephen (Virginia Woolf) con su padre, Sir Leslie Stephen, en 1902. Dos años más tarde, su padre murió y ella se trasladó a Bloomsbury, donde empezó a escribir. El resto de su historia es de sobra conocido.

Adeline Virginia Stephen (Virginia Woolf) con il padre, Sir Leslie Stephen, nel 1902. Due anni più tardi, dopo la morte di suo padre, si trasferì a Bloomsbury e si dedicò alla letteratura. Il resto è un "flusso di coscienza".

10. Fashion
Moda
Moda

The classic hourglass figure. It was the invention of the American illustrator Charles Dana Gibson, and those who forced their bodies into this shape were known as 'Gibson Girls'. Camille Clifford, the owner of this particular classic, was a Danish-born actress.

La clásica silueta denominada "reloj de arena", un invento del ilustrador norteamericano Charles Dana Gibson. Quienes lograban dar esta forma a sus cuerpos recibían el nombre de "chicas Gibson". Camille Clifford, la propietaria de esta clásica figura, era una actriz de origen danés.

La classica figura a vita di vespa, inventata dall'illustratore americano Charles Dana Gibson. Le ragazze che costringevano i loro corpi ad assumere tali forme venivano chiamate "Gibson girl". L'attrice danese Camill Clifford ne è un esempio tipico.

10. Fashion
Moda
Moda

The gloom and restrictions of Victorian times were swept aside by the fashion of the early 1900s. There was a wealth of beautiful materials – velvets, taffetas, *crêpes de Chine*, the softest of wool, the smoothest of cotton, the most delicious silks. There was a wealth of beautiful colour – creams and pinks, flaming reds and deep blues, the gentlest of lilac, the lightest of lavender, and greys that shone with the lustre of silver. There was a plethora of exquisite design – sleeves that dripped with elegance, skirts that hung with grace and style.

There was wealth. There was beauty. Fashion was expensive. Only the rich could afford the abundance of lace and fur, the trimmings of pearl and jet, the threads of gold and the coronets of glimmering jewels. The middle classes starched their cuffs and collars, had their shoes shined and did what they could with cunning and artifice to emulate their well-draped betters. The poor darned and mended their own clothes, and wore their fingers to the bone to make the gorgeous clothes that only the rich would wear.

But the parade of wealth and beauty continued. Actresses, dowagers, débutantes, society beauties and rich young heiresses made sure that they were seen at race meetings, balls, receptions, first nights and photographers' studios in their immaculate and glorious attire.

La tristeza y las limitaciones de la época victoriana fueron pronto barridas por la moda de principios del siglo XX, que contó con una amplia gama de nuevos materiales –como terciopelo, tafetán, crepé chino, lana y algodón de gran suavidad, sedas exquisitas, etc.– y empleó hermosos y variados colores –cremas y rosas, rojos encendidos, azules profundos, suaves lilas, sutiles lavandas y grises que brillaban como la plata–. Los nuevos diseños poseían una gran calidad: mangas colgantes que dotaban a las prendas de elegancia, faldas de caída moderna y estilizada, etc.

Había riqueza. Por tanto, había belleza. La moda era cara, y solo los ricos podían permitirse el lujo de encajes y pieles, el derroche de perlas y azabaches, cadenas de oro y diademas de rutilantes joyas. Las clases medias, en cambio, almidonaban puños y cuellos, se hacían limpiar los zapatos e intentaban emular a base de ingenio y artificio el lujo de sus congéneres más adinerados. Los pobres tenían que conformarse con zurcir y remendar sus ropas de siempre a pesar de ser ellos, con su ingente trabajo, quienes confeccionaban las maravillosas prendas de los ricos.

El desfile de abundancia y belleza parecía no tener fin. Actrices, viudas ricas, debutantes, bellas famosas y jóvenes herederas, ataviadas con sus mejores joyas y vestidos, no dejaban escapar ninguna oportunidad para dejarse ver en todo tipo de lugares y actos sociales, como carreras, bailes, recepciones, estrenos y reuniones en estudios de fotógrafos.

La malinconia e le restrizioni dell'epoca vittoriana furono spazzate via dalla moda dei primi anni del secolo. Un'esplosione di splendidi materiali: velluto, taffetà, crespo di Cina, la lana più soffice, il cotone più morbido, la seta più squisita. Un'esplosione di colori: pastello e rosa, rosso fiammante e azzurro intenso, il violetto più elegante, il lavanda più luminoso, e il grigio che splendeva con la forza dell'argento. Una marea di modelli deliziosi: maniche che cadevano con eleganza, gonne che ondeggiavano con grazia e stile.

La bellezza era accompagnata dalla ricchezza. Vestire alla moda costava caro. Solo i più agiati potevano permettersi di indossare pizzi e pellicce, mettere in mostra perle e giaietti, collane d'oro e tiare scintillanti. La media borghesia sfoggiava colletti e polsini inamidati, calzature lucide e brillanti e faceva il possibile, ricorrendo ad ogni stratagemma, per emulare i personaggi più alla moda. I meno abbienti ricucivano e rammendavano i loro vestiti e si consumavano le mani per realizzare i magnifici vestiti che solo i più ricchi potevano indossare.

Ma la rassegna dei ricchi e dei belli continua: attrici, nobili vedove, debuttanti, bellezze dell'alta società, ereditiere giovani e benestanti facevano di tutto per farsi vedere alle corse, ai balli, ai ricevimenti, alle prime e presso gli studi dei fotografi nelle loro vesti più splendide e immacolate.

(Left) The French actress Gaby Deslys who brought American fashion to Europe. (Opposite) The extravagance of the Folies Bergère, 1905.

(Izquierda) La actriz francesa Gaby Deslys, que introdujo la moda americana en Europa. (Página siguiente) La extravagancia del Folies Bergère, en 1905.

(A sinistra) L'attrice francese Gaby Deslys portò in Europa la moda americana. (Pagina a fianco) La stravaganza delle Folies Bergère, 1905.

In Edwardian times, women's fashions became less bulky and more manageable. This suited their more active lifestyle. It would have been impossible, 50 years earlier, to play croquet in a crinoline.

Durante el reinado de Eduardo VII, la moda femenina perdió en volumen y ganó en comodidad, adaptándose a un estilo de vida más activo. Cincuenta años antes habría sido imposible jugar al *croquet* llevando un vestido de crinolina.

Ai tempi di Edoardo VII, gli indumenti femminili divennero meno ingombranti e più comodi. Era la conseguenza di uno stile di vita più attivo. Sarebbe stato impossibile, mezzo secolo prima, giocare a croquet in crinolina.

The 6th Earl Spencer and his son, Lord Althorp, step out. It was an age when men shone with smartness. Top hats, shoes, lapels, even the ferrules of their umbrellas gleamed. Women had softer styles in sumptuous materials.

El sexto conde de Spencer y su hijo, lord Althorp, caminando a buen paso. En esa época, los hombres vestían con una gran elegancia. Sombreros altos, zapatos, solapas, incluso las puntas de sus paraguas debían brillar. Las mujeres vestían de una forma menos extremada, con materiales suntuosos.

Il sesto conte Spencer e suo figlio, Lord Althorp, vanno a passeggio. In quell'epoca, gli uomini vestivano con grande eleganza. I cilindri, i risvolti delle giacche e perfino i manici dei loro ombrelli brillavano. L'abbigliamento femminile era più morbido, prodotto con materiali sontuosi.

The voluptuous
Edwardian figure
was seen to its full
advantage on stage.
Here are four
members of the
chorus from
The Dairymaids,
24 April 1906.

La voluptuosa
silueta típica de la
época eduardiana
parecía estar hecha
para los escenarios.
En la foto, cuatro
miembros del coro
del espectáculo *The
Dairymaids*, el 24 de
abril de 1906.

La silhouette volut-
tuosa dell'epoca
edoardiana era fatta
apposta per salire in
scena. Nella
fotografia, quattro
membri del coro
dello spettacolo
The Dairymaids,
24 aprile 1906.

(Opposite) The actor Sydney Barraclough, c. 1909. To wear a clean white suit needed a hard-working valet in an age of city smut and grime. (Above) Leslie Stiles and Camille Clifford in a scene from *The Belle of Mayfair*, 11 April 1906.

(Página anterior) El actor Sydney Barraclough, hacia 1909. Lucir un impecable traje blanco representaba un duro trabajo para los criados en una época en que las ciudades estaban llenas de polvo y suciedad. (Arriba) Leslie Stiles y Camille Clifford en una escena de *The Belle of Mayfair*, 11 de abril de 1906.

(Pagina a fianco) L'attore Sydney Barraclough, ca. 1909. Era impossibile indossare un vestito bianco impeccabile senza l'aiuto di un devoto assistente, in un'epoca in cui le città erano sporche e piene di smog. (In alto) Leslie Stiles e Camille Clifford in una scena di *The Belle of Mayfair*, 11 aprile 1906.

Dressed against the elements. (Opposite) Three well-covered paddlers, and (right) a Welsh bathing belle on the beach at Swansea.

Vestidos para la ocasión. (Página anterior) Tres bañistas bien tapados se mojan los pies en el mar. (Derecha) Una joven galesa en la playa de Swansea.

Vestiti contro la forza degli elementi. (Pagina a fianco) Tre bagnanti ben coperti. (A destra) Una "bellezza al bagno" gallese sulla spiaggia di Swansea.

Children were often overdressed. (Left) A young boy in suit and Eton collar, 1900. (Opposite) Miss Kennedy Stott in full regalia, 6 May 1904.

A los pequeños se les solía vestir de forma excesiva. (Izquierda) Un niño con traje y cuello duro, en 1900. (Página siguiente) La señorita Kennedy Stott con sus mejores galas, 6 de mayo de 1904.

Spesso i bambini venivano abbigliati con troppa cura. (A sinistra) Un bambino in abiti eleganti e colletto inamidato, 1900. (Pagina a fianco) Miss Kennedy Stott in tutto il suo splendore, 6 maggio 1904.

Carl and Mark Neaver de Monte in their school uniforms, May 1902. Children well down the social scale worn similar clothes for school, adding discomfort to discipline.

Carl y Mark Neaver de Monte con sus uniformes escolares, en mayo de 1902. Los niños y niñas de clases sociales inferiores también llevaban ropas similares en la escuela, lo que añadía incomodidad a la disciplina.

Carl e Mark Neaver de Monte in uniforme collegiale, maggio 1902. A scuola, anche i bambini delle classi sociali meno agiate indossavano la stessa divisa, sommando la scomodità alla disciplina.

But even at home
there was little
notion of casual
clothes. Master
Trotter poses
for George C
Beresford's camera
in an informal suit,
April 1902.

Ni tan siquiera en
casa se le daba
mucha importancia
a la comodidad. El
señor Trotter posa
para la cámara de
George C. Beresford
vistiendo un traje
informal,
en abril de 1902.

Ma perfino in casa,
non si può certo dire
che si mettessero
comodi. Il piccolo
signor Trotter, in
abiti informali,
posa per il fotografo
George C. Beresford,
aprile 1902.

Even the stiffest of sea breezes would have taken some time to dry these voluminous bathing costumes. In 1909, however, they were the last word in seaside chic, attracting many a roguish eye when filled.

Incluso la más fuerte de las brisas marinas habría tardado en secar estos voluminosos trajes de baño, que en 1909 eran lo último en moda playera y sin duda lograban atraer más de una mirada pícara.

Anche la più forte delle brezze marine ci avrebbe messo del tempo per asciugare questi voluminosi costumi da bagno. Tuttavia, nel 1909, erano l'ultimo grido della moda bagno e attiravano senza dubbio molte occhiate ardenti.

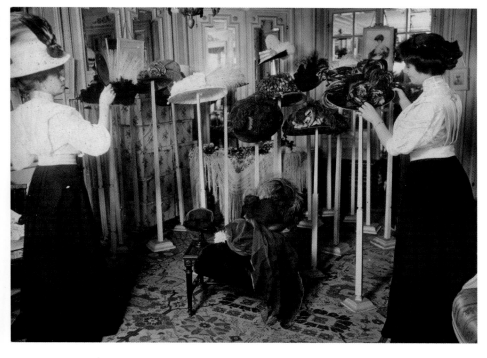

A selection of hats from Maison Corbier at the Exposition des Chapeaux in Paris, 1905. A lady would never be seen without a striking hat. A bare head was a sign of the 'new woman', one who liked both to smoke and vote.

Selección de sombreros de Maison Corbier en la «Exposition des Chapeaux» de París, en 1905. Una verdadera dama nunca salía a la calle sin un sombrero elegante. Solo se atrevían a prescindir del sombrero las "nuevas mujeres", aquellas que además de pedir el voto femenino se atrevían a fumar como los hombres.

Una selezione di cappelli della casa Corbier all'Esposizione di cappelli, Parigi, 1905. Era inammissibile, per una donna, farsi vedere senza un affascinante cappellino. Il capo scoperto era un segno distintivo della "donna moderna", la stessa a cui piaceva fumare e andare a votare.

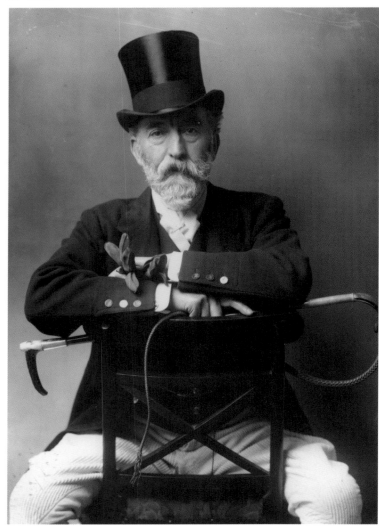

(Left) Memoirs of a foxhunting man. Colonel Douglas Brooke, Master of Foxhounds, 1 May 1902. (Opposite) The actress Phyllis Dare favours ermine, 1905.

(Izquierda) Memorias de un cazador de zorros. El gran cazador de zorros, el coronel Douglas Brooke, el 1 de mayo de 1902. (Página siguiente) La actriz Phyllis Dare prefería el armiño, 1905.

(A sinistra) Memorie di un cacciatore di volpi. Il colonnello Douglas Brooke, maestro nella caccia alla volpe, 1° maggio 1902. (Pagina a fianco) L'attrice Phyllis Dare preferiva gli ermellini, 1905.

11. Science
Ciencia
Scienza

In modern terms it was merely a piece of communications technology. To the early 20th century it was a wonder of science that entered the home. (Right) The British actress Iris Hoey poses beside the telephone, c. 1909.

Hoy es un simple aparato de telecomunicaciones, pero a principios del siglo XX era una maravilla de la ciencia que llevó la tecnología a los hogares. (Derecha) La actriz británica Iris Hoey posa junto a un teléfono, hacia 1909.

Oggi è considerato semplicemente come uno strumento di comunicazione tecnologico, ma ai primi del secolo era visto come una meraviglia della scienza che entrava nelle case. (A destra) L'attrice britannica Iris Hoey posa accanto ad un telefono, ca. 1909.

11. Science
Ciencia
Scienza

Electric-powered machines hummed away, valves flickered, retorts bubbled over the gas jets of Bunsen burners, named after the German chemist who died in 1899. In the early 1900s, research and discovery were in the hands of men and women working at home, in small laboratories with equipment they had made, and on ideas that were their own. And such ideas! In 1900 Max Planck revolutionised physics with the publication of his quantum theory of energy. Five years later Albert Einstein applied Planck's ideas to light and produced his theory of relativity. In 1906 Marie Curie succeeded her husband Pierre as Professor of Physics at the Sorbonne, but much of the work on radium for which they were awarded the Nobel Prize for Physics in 1903 had been done after hours, or at home.

Nations were just beginning to realise how important science was, how carefully scientists should be nurtured, how much investment was needed in new institutes of higher education, how the race was on to be the first, the smartest, the most advanced. Science was becoming a weapon, and gradually the little workshops with their home-made equipment would make way for the gleaming laboratories of large corporations.

El siglo comenzó con ruido de máquinas eléctricas y válvulas y con el burbujeo del gas en los mecheros Bunsen, que reciben su nombre del químico alemán que los inventó, fallecido en 1899. A principios del siglo XX, la investigación y los descubrimientos estaban en manos de hombres y mujeres que trabajaban en casa o en pequeños laboratorios, con material que ellos mismos construían y con ideas y conceptos inauditos hasta entonces. ¡Y qué ideas! En 1900, Max Planck revolucionó la Física con la publicación de su teoría cuántica de la energía, que cinco años más tarde Albert Einstein aplicaría a la luz para obtener su teoría de la relatividad. En 1906, Marie Curie sucedió a su marido Pierre como profesora de Física en la Sorbona, pero la mayor parte de los trabajos sobre el radio por los que recibieron el premio Nobel de Física de 1903 los habían realizado en casa, durante su tiempo libre.

El mundo comenzaba a darse cuenta de la importancia de la ciencia, y los gobiernos vieron que era necesario cuidar a los científicos e invertir en nuevos centros de educación superior para ganar la carrera del conocimiento y el progreso. La ciencia se estaba convirtiendo en un arma, y poco a poco los pequeños laboratorios domésticos dieron paso a las avanzadas instalaciones de las grandes empresas.

Il ronzio degli apparecchi elettrici, il tremolio delle valvole, il ribollire delle storte sui bruciatori a gas dei becchi Bunsen, dal nome del chimico tedesco morto nel 1899. Nei primi anni del secolo, gli esperimenti e le scoperte erano nelle mani di uomini e donne che lavoravano in casa, in piccoli laboratori, fabbricando da sé le attrezzature necessarie e cercando di mettere in pratica idee che appartenevano esclusivamente a loro. E quali idee! Nel 1900, Max Planck rivoluzionava la fisica con la pubblicazione della teoria quantistica dell'energia. Cinque anni dopo, Albert Einstein applicava le teorie di Planck alla luce, formulando la teoria della relatività. Nel 1906, Marie Curie prendeva la cattedra del marito Pierre presso la Facoltà di Fisica della Sorbonne, ma la maggior parte degli studi sulla radioattività, per i quali fu loro assegnato il premio Nobel per la fisica nel 1903, li avevano condotti durante il tempo libero, o a casa.

Le nazioni iniziavano a comprendere l'importanza di coltivare le scienze, di preparare scienziati e ricercatori con la massima attenzione, di investire in nuovi istituti di specializzazione, di essere i primi, i più scaltri, i più avanzati in questa competizione. La scienza stava diventando un'arma e, poco a poco, i locali improvvisati con i loro strumenti artigianali avrebbero dato spazio agli splendenti laboratori delle grandi multinazionali.

Guglielmo Marconi
(extreme left)
watches the
preparation of the
kite that received
the first transatlantic
telegraph signals,
St John's,
Newfoundland,
12 December 1907.

Guglielmo Marconi
(primero por la
izquierda) supervisa
la preparación de la
cometa que recibió
las primeras señales
de telégrafo
procedentes del otro
lado del Atlántico,
St. John, Terranova,
12 de diciembre
de 1907.

Guglielmo Marconi
(sulla sinistra) osserva
la preparazione del
cervo volante che
ha ricevuto i primi
segnali trasmessi
per telegrafo da una
parte all'altra
dell'oceano,
St John's, Terranova,
12 dicembre 1907.

Employees at the Marconi Wireless Telegraph factory in Chelmsford assemble decremeters and wave meters, c. 1909. Marconi's invention was an enormous and immediate financial success.

Empleados de la fábrica de telegrafía sin hilos Marconi, en Chelmsford, montan osciladores y frecuencímetros, hacia 1909. El invento de Marconi se convirtió pronto en un gran éxito económico.

Impiegati della Marconi Wireless Telegraph di Chelmsford impegnati nell'assemblaggio di decremetri e misuratori di onde, ca. 1909. L'invenzione di Marconi ebbe subito un successo economico enorme.

As the telephone and telegraph networks spread, the world was knitted together with a web of wires. An engineer fixes overhead telephone cables above London's Fleet Street, 1907.

A medida que se desplegaban líneas de teléfono y telégrafo, el mundo iba cubriéndose de una verdadera red de hilos. Un ingeniero repara cables de teléfono sobrecalentados en Fleet Street, Londres, 1907.

Il telegrafo ed il telefono si diffondevano rapidamente, mentre l'intero pianeta veniva ricoperto da una fitta rete di cavi. Un tecnico stende dei cavi telefonici su Fleet Street, Londra, 1907.

The first picture transmitted by wire in Germany, 16 May 1907. It was of Emperor Wilhelm II. The transmission took six minutes.

La primera imagen transmitida por cable en Alemania, el 16 de mayo de 1907, era una foto del emperador Guillermo II. La transmisión duró 6 minutos.

La prima immagine trasmessa via cavo in Germania, 16 maggio 1907. È il ritratto dell'imperatore Guglielmo II. La trasmissione durò sei minuti.

The Empire comes together, January 1909. A telegraph operator in London receives a message from India.

El Imperio Británico, más cerca que nunca, en enero de 1909. Un operador de telegrafía recibe en Londres un mensaje enviado desde India.

L'impero britannico sempre più unito, gennaio 1909. A Londra, un operatore del telegrafo riceve un messaggio dall'India.

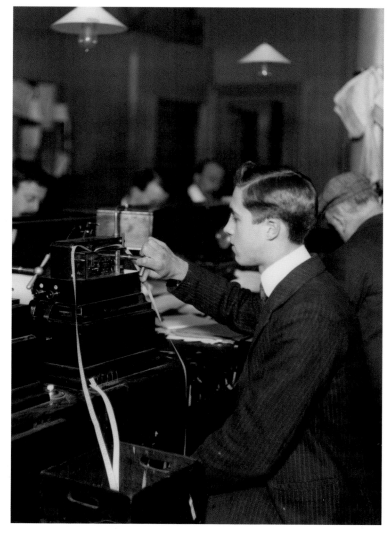

Early protection
against the perils
of fire fighting.
A member of the
London Fire Brigade
with a smoke
helmet, 1908.

Primeras medidas
de seguridad en
la extinción de
incendios. Un
miembro de la
brigada de bomberos
de Londres con un
casco antihumo,
1908.

Primi dispositivi di
protezione contro
i rischi della lotta
contro il fuoco. Un
membro del corpo
dei pompieri di
Londra con una
maschera antifumo,
1908.

Three members of a colliery rescue team with safety lamps and Draeger smoke helmets, 1 March 1908. It was a time of appalling mining disasters all over the world; before long, gas masks would be needed above ground.

Tres miembros de un equipo de rescate con lámparas de seguridad y cascos antihumo Draeger, 1 de marzo de 1908. En aquella época había muchos accidentes mineros en todo el mundo; nadie imaginaba que al cabo de unos años también en la superficie se necesitarían máscaras de gas.

Tre membri della squadra di salvataggio di una miniera di carbone con lanterne di sicurezza e caschi antifumo Draeger, 1° marzo 1908. In quegli anni, nelle miniere di tutto il mondo è un continuo succedersi di tragedie; ben presto le maschere antigas saranno necessarie anche in superficie.

Reinhold Thiele's picture of a woman inside an electric bath at the Light Care Institute, London, c. 1900. The bath was a heavyweight version of a modern sun-bed, and was used for medical reasons.

Foto de Reinhold Thiele de una mujer en un "baño eléctrico" en el Light Care Institute de Londres, hacia 1900. Es una versión antigua de los modernos bronceadores ultravioleta y se utilizaba con fines terapéuticos.

La fotografia di Reinhold Thiele mostra una donna dentro una vasca elettrica del Light Care Institute, Londra, ca. 1900. Lo strano apparecchio è una versione pesante dei moderni lettini a raggi UVA ed era utilizzato per il trattamento di alcune malattie.

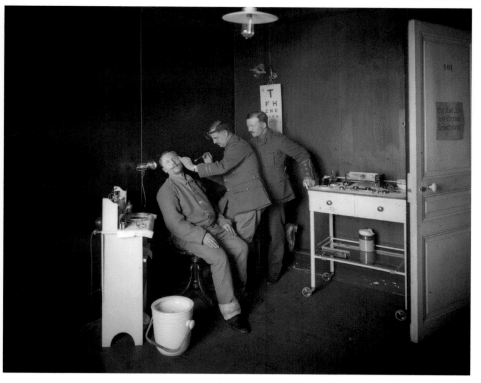

An army hearing test photographed by Thiele, c. 1905. It may be that Tommy Atkins has suffered damage from the noise of an exploding gun, or simply that recruits now faced a more rigorous medical before being accepted.

Prueba de audición en el Ejército, en una foto de Thiele, hacia 1905. Puede que el soldado Tommy Atkins haya sufrido daños debido a una explosión demasiado cercana, o bien que se estén realizando exámenes médicos más rigurosos antes de aceptar a los reclutas.

Prova dell'udito nell'esercito, fotografata da Thiele, ca. 1905. Forse il soldato aveva sofferto dei danni al timpano a causa di un'esplosione, o più semplicemente ora, per arruolarsi, era necessario passare una visita medica più rigorosa.

The German-born mathematical physicist Albert Einstein, 1905. It was the year of the publication of his theory of relativity.

El físico y matemático de origen alemán Albert Einstein hacia 1905, el año en que publicó su teoría de la relatividad.

Il matematico e fisico tedesco Albert Einstein, 1905. Era l'anno in cui pubblicò la sua teoria della relatività.

The Polish-born physicist Marie Curie in her laboratory in Paris, c. 1909. She was working on the isolation of pure radium.

Marie Curie, de origen polaco, en su laboratorio de París, hacia 1909, donde trabajaba en el aislamiento del radio puro.

Il premio Nobel per la fisica di origine polacca Marie Curie, nel suo laboratorio parigino, ca. 1909. Stava cercando di isolare il radio allo stato puro.

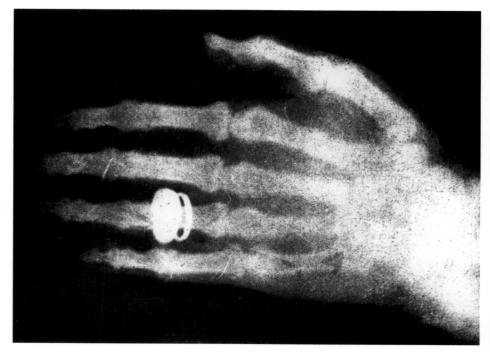

(Opposite) The German physicist Wilhelm Conrad Röntgen, 1906.
His discovery of X-rays won him the Nobel Prize for Physics in 1901.
(Above) One of Röntgen's first X-ray pictures – his wife's hand.

(Página siguiente) El físico alemán Wilhelm Conrad Röntgen, 1906.
El descubrimiento de los rayos X le valió el premio Nobel de Física
de 1901. (Arriba) Una de las primeras imágenes de rayos X obtenida
por Röntgen: la mano de su esposa.

(Pagina a fianco) Il fisico tedesco Wilhelm Conrad Röntgen, 1906.
La sua scoperta dei raggi X gli fece guadagnare il premio Nobel
per la fisica nel 1901. (In alto) Una delle prime immagini a raggi X
di Röntgen: la mano di sua moglie.

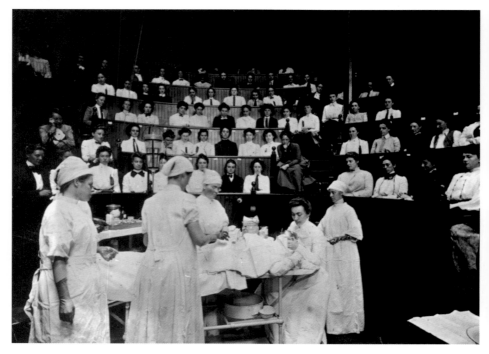

Florence Nightingale takes over. American women doctors perform an operation in front of a lecture theatre full of students, November 1907. Some men were amused, others horrified. The patient was grateful.

Florence Nightingale se dispone a operar. Doctoras americanas realizan una intervención en un aula llena de estudiantes, noviembre de 1907. Algunos hombres mostraban interés, otros no podían ocultar su espanto, pero el paciente tenía mucho que agradecerles.

Florence Nightingale al comando. Dottoresse americane eseguono un'operazione in un auditorium pieno di studenti di medicina, novembre 1907. Alcuni uomini sorridevano, altri erano terrorizzati. Il paziente è rimasto contento.

A medical assistant
in protective
clothing prepares
to take an X-ray,
March 1909. The
patient was terrified.

Un auxiliar médico
con ropa protectora
se dispone a hacer
una radiografía,
marzo de 1909.
El paciente estaba
asustadísimo.

Un medico assistente
con indumenti di
protezione si prepara
per effettuare una
radiografia, marzo
1909. Il paziente
moriva di paura.

The Lavery Electric Automatic Phrenometer whirrs into action, August 1907. It measured the activity of the brain. This is the portable version.

El "frenómetro eléctrico automático" de Lavery, que servía para medir la actividad cerebral, agosto de 1907. En la foto aparece la versión portátil de este aparato.

Il Frenometro automatico elettronico di Lavery entra in azione, agosto 1907. Serviva a misurare l'attività cerebrale. Questa è la versione portatile.

A penny-in-the-slot boot and shoe-polishing machine, November 1907. It was noisier than a boot boy but did not require a tip.

Un máquina para limpiar zapatos, noviembre de 1907. Era más ruidosa que un limpiabotas pero no exigía propina.

Una macchina lustrascarpe a monete, novembre 1907. Faceva più rumore di un lustrascarpe normale ma non chiedeva la mancia.

Switchboard operators at the Manchester Telephone Exchange, c. 1900. The supervisors are seated in the centre aisle.

Operadoras de la central telefónica de Manchester, hacia 1900. Los supervisores están sentados en la zona central.

Operatrici in azione presso la centrale telefonica di Manchester controllate dai supervisori che siedono alle loro spalle, ca. 1900.

12. Transport
   Transporte
   Mezzi di trasporto

A brief period of co-existence before the New drove the Old off the road. A motor cab overtakes a horse-drawn hansom on a city street, July 1907. The days of nipping into the road for a shovelful of manure for the garden were numbered.

Un breve período de coexistencia antes de que lo nuevo desplazara a lo viejo. Un taxi adelanta a un coche de caballos, julio de 1907. La época en que uno podía salir a la calle y recoger una palada de estiércol para el jardín tenía los días contados.

Un breve periodo di convivenza prima che le novità prendessero il posto delle anticaglie. Una macchina supera una carrozzella in una strada cittadina, luglio 1907. I tempi in cui ci si precipitava in strada a raccogliere una palata di concime per il giardino stavano per terminare.

12. Transport
Transporte
Mezzi di trasporto

When the inaugural train opened the Paris Métro in 1900, it carried one passenger. There were no celebratory fireworks, no banquets, no speeches, no bands. One of the city's aldermen prophesied total failure for the scheme. He wondered who would want to use it.

Within a few years millions of passengers had allayed his fears. They flocked to the Métro as they did to the new Berlin Underground in 1902, the extensions to the London system, and the New York City subway in 1904. Above ground too, all was change. Railways enjoyed one last boom before they reached saturation point. There were electric buses, trams, taxis and elevated railways. Products of the great names in motoring – Daimler, Benz, Rolls and Royce, Panhard, De Dion, Ford, Renault and dozens more – hummed and rattled along the streets. Horse-drawn vehicles had a few more years in service, but the internal combustion engine was already master of the road.

Strange new contraptions took to the skies. The Wright brothers achieved the first flight by a heavier-than-air machine in 1903, three years after the first Zeppelin had loomed over Germany. Before the decade was out, Louis Blériot had flown over the Channel.

El tren que inauguró el metro de París, en 1900, llevaba un solo pasajero. La celebración no tuvo fuegos artificiales, banquetes, discursos ni música. Uno de los concejales del ayuntamiento profetizó un total fracaso para el nuevo medio de transporte. ¿Quién iba a utilizarlo?

Al cabo de pocos años, millones de pasajeros se encargaron de desmentirle. La gente utilizaba el metro parisino con toda normalidad, y lo mismo ocurrió con el nuevo metro de Berlín, de 1902, las ampliaciones del metro de Londres y el metro de Nueva York, inaugurado en 1904. Tanto bajo tierra como en la superficie, las cosas estaban cambiando.

El ferrocarril vivió una época de esplendor antes de saturarse. Pronto hubo autobuses eléctricos, tranvías, taxis y trenes elevados. Las calles se llenaron de vehículos con célebres nombres: Daimler, Benz, Rolls Royce, Panhard, De Dion, Ford, Renault, etc. Los carros de caballos aún prestarían servicio durante varios años, pero el motor de combustión interna ya era el rey de la carretera.

Nuevos y extraños artilugios invadieron los cielos. Los hermanos Wright realizaron el primer vuelo en un artefacto más pesado que el aire en 1903, tres años después de que el primer dirigible sobrevolara Alemania. Antes del fin de la década, Louis Blériot cruzó el canal de la Mancha.

Il primo treno che inaugurò il servizio metropolitano parigino nel 1900 trasportava solo un passeggero. Niente fuochi di artificio per l'inaugurazione, nessun banchetto, nessun discorso, nessuna banda. Uno dei consiglieri comunali aveva profetizzato un fallimento totale per il nuovo servizio, domandandosi chi mai avrebbe voluto farne uso.

Nel giro di pochi anni, milioni di utenti avevano placato le sue paure, affollandosi nel Métro francese così come nella metropolitana di Berlino nel 1902, nelle estensioni della rete londinese e nella Subway di New York nel 1904. Anche in superficie tutto stava cambiando. Le ferrovie vivevano un ultimo periodo di espansione prima di raggiungere un punto di saturazione. C'erano autobus elettrici, tram, taxi e treni sopraelevati. Le proposte dei grandi nomi dell'industria automobilistica – Daimler, Benz, Rolls Royce, Panhard, De Dion, Ford, Renault e molti altri – sfrecciavano con fragore per le vie delle città. I veicoli trainati da cavalli avrebbero tirato avanti per qualche anno, ma il motore a scoppio si era ormai impadronito delle strade.

Nuovi marchingegni sfidavano i cieli. I fratelli Wright furono i primi a volare con una macchina più pesante dell'aria nel 1903, mentre tre anni prima il primo dirigibile aveva sorvolato la Germania. Prima della fine del decennio, Louis Blériot sarebbe riuscito a superare il Canale della Manica.

Trademark of the 20th century. Watched by his brother Wilbur, Orville Wright takes to the air in his 12hp heavier-than-air machine from the sands of Kill Devil Hills, Kitty Hawk, North Carolina, 17 December 1903.

El símbolo del siglo XX. Bajo la mirada de su hermano Wilbur, Orville Wright despega en su artefacto más pesado que el aire, de 12 caballos de potencia, desde la pista de Kill Devil Hills, en Kitty Hawk, Carolina del Norte, el 17 de diciembre de 1903.

Il marchio del XX secolo. Sotto lo sguardo del fratello Wilbur, Orville Wright spicca il volo su un apparecchio a 12 CV più pesante dell'aria, dalle spiagge di Kill Devil Hills, Kitty Hawk, Carolina del Nord, 17 dicembre 1903.

Touring the towers. (Opposite) The Italian airship *Parsival* is moored to the Campanile in the Piazza San Marco, Venice, c. 1909. (Above) Count Charles de Lambert circles the Eiffel Tower, 18 October 1909.

Sobrevolando las torres. (Página anterior) El dirigible italiano *Parsival* amarrado al Campanile de la plaza de San Marcos, Venecia, hacia 1909. (Arriba) El conde Charles de Lambert sobrevuela la Torre Eiffel, el 18 de octubre de 1909.

Visita alle torri. (Pagina a fianco) Il dirigibile italiano *Parsival* ormeggia sul campanile di Piazza San Marco a Venezia, ca. 1909. (In alto) Il conte Charles de Lambert esegue un giro intorno alla torre Eiffel, 18 ottobre 1909.

British royalty. Seated in the 12hp Panhard are (from left to right): Sir Charles Cust, royal equerry; Lord Llangattock and his son the Hon. C S Rolls (of Rolls-Royce); and the Duke of York (later George V). The date is 1900.

La realeza británica. Sentados en este Panhard de 12 caballos, de izquierda a derecha: Sir Charles Cust, caballerizo real; lord Llangattock y su hijo, el honorable C. S. Rolls (de Rolls Royce) y el duque de York (el futuro Jorge V). Corría el año 1900.

I reali britannici. Seduti sulla 12 CV Panhard da sinistra a destra: Sir Charles Cust, scudiero reale; Lord Llangattock e figlio, l'onorevole C. S. Rolls (fondatore della Rolls-Royce); per ultimo, il duca di York (futuro Giorgio V), 1900.

American aristocracy. Henry Ford lounges in the comfort of his latest model, outside his own factory, c. 1905. The Model T and assembly-line mass production were only three years away.

Aristocracia americana. Henry Ford comprueba la comodidad de su último modelo, en el exterior de su fábrica, hacia 1905. El Ford T y la producción en serie solo tardarían tres años en llegar.

L'aristocrazia americana. Henry Ford si mette comodo sul suo ultimo modello davanti alla fabbrica di sua proprietà, ca. 1905. Il Modello T e le catene di montaggio erano solo a tre anni di distanza.

A survivor from
an earlier age.
One of the last
penny farthing
cycles crosses
Hammersmith
Bridge, London,
1900.

Un superviviente
de otra época.
Uno de los últimos
biciclos cruzando
el puente de
Hammersmith,
Londres, 1900.

Un sopravvissuto dei
tempi passati. Uno
degli ultimi bicicli
attraversa il ponte
di Hammersmith,
Londra, 1900.

Becoming acquainted. Her Ladyship gives one of her greys
a reassuring pat, 1904. These horses need not have worried –
they would have been kept on for ceremonial occasions.
For others, the knacker's yard beckoned.

La hora de las presentaciones. Desde su automóvil, una
dama acaricia a uno de sus caballos, que no tenían por qué
preocuparse, pues seguirían participando en las grandes
ocasiones, 1904. Otros caballos no correrían la misma suerte.

Stringendo amicizia. Sua Eccellenza concede una carezza
rassicurante ad uno dei suoi cavalli, 1904. Non c'era motivo di
preoccupazione per questi equini, ancora avevano molto da fare
nelle cerimonie ufficiali. Per altri, la destinazione era il macello.

Alfred Hind Robinson's majestic panorama of the
Flying Scotsman heading north over the railway bridge
at Berwick-upon-Tweed, 29 May 1903. These were the
early days of the 'crack' expresses.

Una bella imagen de Alfred Hind Robinson: el *Flying
Scotsman* cruzando el puente de Berwick-upon-Tweed
en dirección al norte, el 29 de mayo de 1903. Eran los
primeros tiempos de los grandes expresos.

Un maestoso panorama di Alfred Hind Robinson: il
Flying Scotsman si dirige a nord attraverso il ponte di
Berwick-upon-Tweed, 29 maggio 1903. Erano i primi
tempi dei "velocissimi" treni espresso.

Crowds gather to
watch the fire brigade
deal with a derail-
ment on the Berlin
overhead railway,
September 1907.

Curiosos y una
brigada de
bomberos en un
descarrilamiento
de un tren elevado
en Berlín, septiembre
de 1907.

Un gruppo di gente si
ferma ad osservare i
pompieri accorsi per
un deragliamento
sulla sopraelevata
di Berlino, settembre
1907.

The tangled wreckage of the Zeppelin airship LZ 4 after it caught fire at Echterdingen, 3 August 1908. The airship was the fourth to be constructed by Count Ferdinand von Zeppelin.

Los restos del dirigible LZ 4 después de sufrir un incendio en Echterdingen, el 3 de agosto de 1908. Era el cuarto que construía el conde Ferdinand von Zeppelin.

Il groviglio di rottami del dirigibile LZ4 dopo il suo incendio ad Echterdingen, 3 agosto 1908. Era il quarto aerostato costruito dal conte Ferdinand von Zeppelin.

The Brennan monorail has a day out, May 1907. The monorail was designed by Louis Brennan, but initially many scoffed at its toy-like appearance. (Above) Brennan's son negotiates a suspended cable.

El monorraíl Brennan en pleno viaje, mayo de 1907. Fue diseñado por Louis Brennan, y al principio muchos se reían de su invento por tener el aspecto de un juguete. (Arriba) El hijo de Brennan se desplaza por un cable suspendido.

Il monorotaia Brennan in azione, maggio 1907. All'inizio, il marchingegno disegnato da Louis Brennan era oggetto di scherno a causa del suo aspetto di giocattolo. (In alto) Il figlio di Brennan su un cavo sospeso.

Bert Colver rides his 3.5hp Matchless at an Essex Motor Club meeting, 8 August 1908. The motorcycle was the steed for the new knight of the road – fast, reliable (sometimes), dangerous and totally exhilarating.

Bert Colver en su Matchless de 3,5 caballos en un encuentro en el Essex Motor Club, el 8 de agosto de 1908. La motocicleta era el corcel de los nuevos jinetes de la carretera: rápida, fiable (a veces), peligrosa y muy emocionante.

Bert Colver sulla sua 3,5 CV Matchless ad un raduno dell'Essex Motor Club, 8 agosto 1908. La motocicletta era il destriero dei nuovi cavalieri della strada: rapida, affidabile (a volte), pericolosa e assolutamente divertente.

An early ancestor of the tanks of the First World War. Rustin and Hornby of Lincoln manufactured this caterpillar-track farm machine in 1902. The plough horse was about to join the cab horse in the ranks of the unemployed.

Un ancestro de los tanques de la Primera Guerra Mundial. Rustin y Hornby de Lincoln fabricaron en 1902 esta máquina agrícola de tracción por cadenas. El caballo de tiro estaba a punto de unirse a los caballos de los carruajes en la cola del paro.

Un antico parente dei carri armati della Prima guerra mondiale. Rustin e Hornby di Lincoln avevano fabbricato questo trattore a cingoli nel 1902. Il cavallo da tiro stava per raggiungere i suoi colleghi di città nella lista dei disoccupati.

Henry Farman flies his
Voisin-Farman biplane over
1km, Issy-les-Moulineaux,
13 January 1908, and wins
the 50,000-franc Deutsch-
Archdeacon prize.

Henry Farman hace volar su
biplano Voisin-Farman a lo
largo de 1 km de distancia en
Issy-les-Moulineaux, el 13 de
enero de 1908, y se lleva los
50.000 francos del premio
Deutsch-Archdeacon.

Henry Farman percorre un
chilometro sul suo biplano
Voisin-Farman a Issy-les
Moulineaux e vince i
50.000 franchi del premio
Deutsch-Archdeacon,
13 gennaio 1908.

Overground luxury. The interior of the buffet saloon car on the Great Western Railway, c. 1900. No expense was spared on the fittings – plush upholstery, mahogany panelling, moulded ceilings.

Lujo en la superficie. El interior del coche restaurante del Great Western Railway, hacia 1900. Al menos en los acabados no se había reparado en gastos: tapicería suntuosa, paneles de caoba y techos con molduras.

Lusso in superficie. L'interno del vagone ristorante-salotto della Great Western Railway, ca. 1900. Per l'arredamento non si badava a spese: tappezzeria di lusso, pannelli in mogano e soffitti lavorati.

Underground functionalism. One of the passenger tunnels at Hampstead Station on the newly-opened Northern Line extension of the London Underground, 1909. The line connected the City with the wealthy suburbs of north London.

Funcionalismo bajo tierra. Uno de los túneles para pasajeros de la estación de Hampstead, en la recién inaugurada ampliación de la línea Norte del metro de Londres, en 1909, que conectaba la City con los barrios residenciales del norte de la ciudad.

Funzionalismo sotterraneo. Uno dei tunnel di transito della stazione di Hampstead, sulla nuova Northern Line, prolungamento della rete metropolitana di Londra, 1909. La linea collegava la City con i ricchi sobborghi residenziali a nord della città.

13. Sport
Deporte
Sport

Goldsmith and Hewitt, in unlikely costume, exhibit illegal bare-knuckle skills in a carpeted room against a painted background, 1908. Even if the camera could not lie, it might attempt to deceive.

Goldsmith y Hewitt, vestidos de una forma poco habitual, muestran sus habilidades en boxeo sin guantes, un deporte ilegal, ante un fondo pintado, 1908. Aunque la cámara no mienta, sí puede engañar.

Goldsmith e Hewitt, con dei costumi inverosimili, combattono illegalmente a mani nude in una stanza con il pavimento tappezzato e uno sfondo dipinto, 1908. La macchina fotografica non poteva mentire, ma poteva provare ad ingannare.

13. Sport
Deporte
Sport

Never before had sport been so popular. Throughout the world crowds swarmed to stadiums, arenas, parks, clubs and race tracks. There were international matches and competitions in soccer, rugby, tennis, golf, athletics, motor racing and a dozen more manly (and, to an increasing degree, womanly) recreations. The first Davis Cup (tennis) tournament took place in 1900; the first Tour de France in 1903; the first rugby international between France and England and the first motor race at Le Mans in 1906.

Nations, states and cities competed with each other in newly-formed leagues and championships. To fans all over the world what mattered was 'victory'. When its local team won, a whole town celebrated. When a country lost, national pride suffered.

There were occasions when an entire race seemed bent on proving its superiority. In 1908 Jack Johnson became the first black boxer to be crowned World Heavyweight Champion. The hunt was immediately on to find the 'Great White Hope', a fighter capable of taking the title from Johnson. The man chosen was James J Jeffries, an ex-sparring partner of Gentleman Jim Corbett. Jeffries came out of retirement at the age of 35 to fight Johnson. But that fight came in the next decade…

El deporte nunca había sido tan popular. En todo el mundo, las multitudes acudían a estadios, circuitos, parques, clubes y pistas de carreras. Se celebraban encuentros y competiciones internacionales de fútbol, *rugby*, tenis, golf, atletismo y motor, entre muchas otras especialidades, la mayoría de ellas masculinas pero con una participación femenina cada vez más importante. La primera Copa Davis de tenis se celebró en 1900, en 1903 tuvo lugar el primer Tour de Francia, y en 1906 se disputaron el primer encuentro internacional de *rugby* entre Francia e Inglaterra y la primera carrera automovilística de Le Mans.

Se crearon ligas y campeonatos en los que participaban varios países y ciudades, y para los aficionados de todo el mundo, la palabra clave era "victoria". Cuando ganaba el equipo local, la fiesta estaba garantizada, mientras que las derrotas se vivían como un duro golpe para el orgullo nacional.

En ocasiones, las competiciones deportivas parecían pruebas de superioridad. Por ejemplo, en 1908 Jack Johnson se convirtió en el primer boxeador de raza negra en ganar el campeonato mundial de pesos pesados. Inmediatamente se empezó a buscar a la "gran esperanza blanca" que pudiera arrebatarle el título, y el elegido fue James J. Jeffries, antiguo *sparring* de Jim Corbett. Jeffries, ya retirado a sus 35 años, volvió al cuadrilátero para luchar contra Johnson, pero el encuentro se demoraría hasta la siguiente década…

Gli sport non erano mai stati così popolari. Gli stadi, le arene, i parchi, i club e le piste di tutto il mondo erano sempre pieni di gente che accorreva ad assistere a incontri e gare internazionali di calcio, rugby, tennis, golf, atletica, automobilismo e motociclismo e numerose altre competizioni maschili e, in misura sempre crescente, femminili. Il primo torneo della Coppa Davis di tennis ebbe luogo nel 1900; il primo Tour de France nel 1903; il primo scontro di rugby tra la Francia e l'Inghilterra e la prima corsa automobilistica di Le Mans nel 1906.

Città e nazioni si sfidavano le une contro le altre in nuovi campionati e tornei. Per i tifosi di tutto il mondo l'importante era "vincere". Se una squadra locale trionfava, tutta la città si abbandonava ai festeggiamenti; se i rappresentanti di un paese perdevano, l'orgoglio nazionale veniva duramente ferito.

In alcune occasioni, si tirava in ballo perfino la superiorità di una razza intera. Nel 1908 Jack Johnson fu il primo pugile di colore ad ottenere la corona di campione del mondo dei pesi massimi. Immediatamente iniziò la caccia alla "grande speranza bianca", un uomo che riuscisse a strappare il titolo a Johnson. La scelta ricadde su James J. Jeffries, ex-allenatore di boxe del "gentlemen" Jim Corbett. Jeffries, che si era ritirato, tornò sul ring all'età di 35 anni per sfidare Johnson. Ma il grande match appartiene alla storia del decennio seguente…

Pat Ewry of the United States practises for the standing high jump at the
London Olympic Games, 1 July 1908. In the Games themselves, Ewry won
gold medals for this event, the standing long jump and the standing triple jump.

El estadounidense Pat Ewry se entrena para la prueba de salto de altura durante
los Juegos Olímpicos de París, 1 de julio de 1908. Durante los Juegos, Ewry
ganó el oro en esta especialidad y también en salto de longitud y triple salto.

Lo statunitense Pat Ewry si allena per una gara di salto in alto da fermo ai
Giochi Olimpici di Londra, 1° luglio 1908. In quella occasione, Ewry vinse
la medaglia d'oro in tutte e tre le prove di salto da fermo, in alto, in lungo
e triplo.

Alfred Shrubb of Great Britain, one of the best long distance runners of the early 20th century, c. 1909.

El británico Alfred Shrubb, uno de los mejores fondistas de principios del siglo XX, hacia 1909.

Il britannico Alfred Shrubb, uno dei migliori corridori di fondo dei primi anni del secolo, ca. 1909.

John Taylor of the United States poses for a press camera in front of the empty seats of the White City Stadium, July 1908. Taylor was competing in the quarter mile event at the London Olympics.

El estadounidense John Taylor posa para la prensa ante los asientos vacíos del estadio White City, en julio de 1908. Taylor compitió en la prueba del cuarto de milla durante los Juegos Olímpicos de Londres.

John Taylor, degli Stati Uniti, in posa per la stampa di fronte alle tribune vuote del White City Stadium, luglio 1908. Doveva partecipare alla corsa del quarto di miglio (ca. 400 metri) delle Olimpiadi di Londra.

One of the team of Danish women gymnasts limbers up for the London Olympics, July 1908. It was an event the Danes dominated.

Una de las gimnastas del equipo danés se prepara para los Juegos Olímpicos de Londres, en julio de 1908. Las danesas dominaban en esta especialidad.

Una delle ginnaste della rappresentazione danese esegue esercizi di riscaldamento alle Olimpiadi di Londra, luglio 1908. La squadra danese dominò la competizione.

Canadian Robert Carr
(extreme right) wins the final
of the 100-yard sprint at the
British Amateur Athletic
Association Championships
at the White City, London,
July 1908. Second was
Robert Walker of South
Africa (third from right).

El canadiense Robert Carr
(primero por la derecha)
gana la final de los
100 metros lisos durante
los campeonatos de la
Asociación Británica de
Atletismo Amateur, en
Londres, julio de 1908.
La plata fue para el
sudafricano Robert
Walker (tercero por
la derecha).

Il canadese Robert Carr
(l'ultimo a destra) vince la
finale dei cento metri piani
durante i campionati
amatoriali della British
Athletic Association al White
City di Londra, luglio 1908.
Il secondo fu il sudafricano
Robert Walker (il terzo a
partire da destra).

Not the last cavalry charge in British history, but a disastrous moment as jockeys and mounts come down to earth in the Grand National at Aintree racecourse, Liverpool.

No se trata de la última carga de la caballería británica, sino de un momento fatal en que jinetes y caballos chocan y caen al suelo durante el Grand National, en el estadio de Aintree, en Liverpool.

Non si tratta dell'ultima carica di cavalleria della storia britannica, ma piuttosto di un momento tragico in cui cavalli e fantini cadono a terra sulla pista di Aintree, durante il Grand National a Liverpool.

The Sport of Kings, but apparently not of gentlemen. The English upper classes enjoy a day at the races, while a young woman hugs her feather boa and waits for attention. And all this at Ascot!

El deporte de los reyes, pero aparentemente no para caballeros. Las clases altas inglesas disfrutan de un día en las carreras, mientras una joven juega con su boa de plumas esperando que alguien le preste atención. El escenario es el estadio de Ascot.

Lo sport dei re, ma a quanto pare non quello dei gentlemen. L'alta borghesia inglese si gode una giornata alle corse, mentre una ragazza stringe il suo boa di piume in attesa che qualcuno le presti un po' di attenzione. E il tutto ad Ascot!

Another section of the crowd at Ascot on 1 June 1907. Ascot was the most important race meeting on the social calendar. One simply had to be seen there, looking one's best and hobnobbing with all the right people.

Otra zona del público, también en Ascot, el 1 de junio de 1907. En Ascot se celebraba la carrera de caballos más importante de la temporada. Bastaba con dejarse ver y vestir con la elegancia necesaria para disfrutar de la compañía de la gente bien.

Un altro gruppo di spettatori ad Ascot, 1° giugno 1907. Le corse di cavalli ad Ascot costituivano l'evento sociale più atteso del calendario sportivo. L'importante era farsi vedere lì, vestiti con la massima eleganza e con la giusta compagnia.

Alfred Trott of Middlesex County Cricket Club bowling on a practice ground. Trott was also a batsman of considerable talent, and is the only cricketer to have hit a ball over the Pavilion at Lord's.

Alfred Trott, del club de *cricket* Middlesex County, lanzando la bola en un campo de entrenamiento. Trott era también un buen bateador y tenía el récord de haber lanzado la bola por encima del pabellón de Lord.

Alfred Trott, del circolo sportivo di cricket della contea di Middlesex, si esibisce in un lancio su un campo di allenamento. Trott era anche un battitore di grande talento ed è l'unico giocatore di cricket ad aver spedito una palla oltre il padiglione del campo di Lord.

The Father of
Modern Cricket.
Dr William Gilbert
Grace was still in his
prime when this
photograph was
taken in 1900.

El padre del
cricket moderno.
El Dr. William
Gilbert estaba
todavía en su
mejor forma
cuando se tomó
esta foto, en 1900.

Il capostipite del
cricket moderno.
Il dottor William
Gilbert Grace era
al culmine della sua
carriera quando, nel
1900, gli fu scattata
questa fotografia.

The trophy table at the Richmond Horse Show, 14 June 1907.
Then, as now, Richmond was always a most law-abiding place,
and the policeman on guard is clearly bored out of his skull.

La mesa de los trofeos en el Richmond Horse Show, 14 de
junio de 1907. Entonces, como ahora, en Richmond se
respetaban las leyes escrupulosamente, y los policías, como
el de la foto, más bien se aburrían.

Il tavolo dei trofei al Richmond Horse Show, 14 giugno 1907.
Allora come oggi, Richmond è sempre un luogo in cui si
osserva scrupolosamente la legge e pare che il poliziotto
di guardia si stia annoiando a morte.

In the days before indecipherable public address systems, spectators relied on the inaudible voice of the City toastmaster to keep them up to date with what was happening at the London Olympics of 1908.

Con un sistema de megafonía propio de la época, los espectadores tenían que confiar en la inaudible voz del maestro de ceremonias para mantenerse al corriente de lo que pasaba en los Juegos Olímpicos de 1908.

Prima dell'avvento degli incomprensibili sistemi di amplificazione degli stadi, gli spettatori dovevano accontentarsi della voce impercettibile del maestro di cerimonie per tenersi al corrente di ciò che succedeva alle Olimpiadi di Londra del 1908.

The man who came second but won the gold medal: John Hayes of the USA completes the Olympic marathon, 24 July 1908.

El hombre que llegó segundo pero ganó la medalla de oro: el estadounidense John Hayes alcanza la meta en la maratón olímpica, el 24 de julio de 1908.

L'uomo che arrivò secondo e vinse la medaglia d'oro: lo statunitense John Hayes taglia il traguardo della maratona olimpica, 24 luglio 1908.

Triumph to tragedy. Dorando Pietri of Italy is helped across the finishing line in the same marathon and is subsequently disqualified. He had entered the stadium well ahead of Hayes, but in his confused exhaustion had turned the wrong way. His assistant in the tweeds is the writer Sir Arthur Conan Doyle.

Del triunfo a la tragedia. En la misma maratón, el italiano Dorando Pietri es descalificado por recibir ayuda al cruzar la meta. Había entrado en el estadio con bastante ventaja sobre Hayes, pero el cansancio hizo que se equivocara de trazado. Su auxiliar, con traje de lana, es ni más ni menos que el escritor sir Arthur Conan Doyle.

Dal trionfo alla tragedia. L'italiano Dorando Pietri viene aiutato sulla linea di meta della stessa maratona ed è squalificato. Era entrato nello stadio molto prima di Hayes, ma era talmente esausto che, nella confusione, aveva svoltato a destra anziché a sinistra. L'uomo in tweed che lo assiste è lo scrittore Sir Arthur Conan Doyle.

Bob Fitzsimmons, c.1900. Fitzsimmons was the first fighter to win three world titles – middleweight (1891), heavyweight (1897) and light-heavyweight (1903).

Bob Fitzsimmons, hacia 1900. Fitzsimmons fue el primer luchador que ganó tres títulos mundiales: pesos medio (1891), pesados (1897) y semipesados (1903).

Bob Fitzsimmons, ca. 1900. È stato il primo pugile che ha vinto tre titoli mondiali in categorie differenti: pesi medi (1891), pesi massimi (1897) e mediomassimi (1903).

Reinhold Thiele's portrait of the American boxer James J Jeffries, c. 1900. Jeffries had taken the world heavyweight title from Fitzsimmons a year earlier.

Retrato de Reinhold Thiele del boxeador americano James J. Jeffries, hacia 1900. El año anterior, Jeffries había arrebatado a Fitzsimmons el título mundial de pesos pesados.

Un ritratto di Reinhold Thiele del pugile statunitense James J. Jeffries, ca. 1900. Un anno prima, Jeffries aveva strappato il titolo di campione del mondo dei pesi massimi a Fitzsimmons.

Sumo wrestlers in action, 1909. Following the heroic Japanese victory in the
war against Russia, there was a craze in the West for all things Japanese – furniture,
music, costume, decoration and martial arts. And sumo? Who knows?

Luchadores de sumo en acción, en 1909. Tras la heroica victoria japonesa en la guerra
contra Rusia, todo lo japonés se puso de moda en Occidente: muebles, música, vestidos,
decoración, artes marciales ¿y también el sumo?

Lottatori di sumo in azione, 1909. Dopo l'eroica vittoria giapponese nella guerra contro
la Russia, gli occidentali impazzivano per qualsiasi cosa proveniente dal paese del Sol
Levante: mobili, musica, abbigliamento, decorazioni ed arti marziali. E il sumo, chissà?

Time-out from the playing fields of Eton, c. 1900. The Eton soccer team psyching itself up before an important game. One hopes that they calmed down before play started.

Tiempo muerto en el campo de deportes de Eton, en 1900. El equipo de fútbol de Eton se concentra antes de un importante encuentro. Era fundamental salir al campo con mentalidad de ganador.

Time out nel campo di calcio di Eton, ca. 1900. La squadra locale cerca l'ispirazione prima di un importante incontro. C'era da sperare che i giocatori trovassero la calma prima dell'inizio della partita.

A women's
volleyball game,
1900. The setting
is almost certainly a
college somewhere
in the United States.

Un partido
de voleibol
femenino,
en 1900,
probablemente
en un centro
educativo de
Estados Unidos.

Una partita di
pallavolo femminile,
1900. Lo scenario
è quasi sicuramente
quello di una scuola
da qualche parte
negli Stati Uniti.

A smoky start to
the Indianapolis
100-Mile Race at the
Speedway, c. 1909.
By this time cars
were capable
of 100mph.

Una nube de humo
en la salida de las
100 millas de
Indianápolis, en
Speedway, hacia
1909. Los coches
de carreras de esa
época alcanzaban
los 160 km/h.

Una nuvola di fumo
alla partenza della
Cento Miglia sul
circuito di
Indianapolis, ca.
1909. All'epoca le
macchine potevano
raggiungere una
velocità di 160 km/h.

Body puncher.
Frederick Grace, the
British lightweight
boxer who won the
Olympic gold medal
in London in the
summer of 1908.

Un gran boxeador.
Frederick Grace, el
peso ligero británico
que ganó la medalla
de oro olímpica en
Londres en el verano
de 1908.

Un gran picchiatore.
Frederick Grace,
il pugile britannico
che vinse la
medaglia d'oro
dei pesi leggeri
alle Olimpiadi di
Londra, nell'estate
del 1908.

Body builder.
Reinhold Thiele's
portrait of
Mr Murray,
proud winner
of the Sandow
bodybuilding
competition, 1905.

Todo músculos.
Retrato de Reinhold
Thiele de Mr.
Murray, campeón
de la competición
de culturismo de
Sandow, en 1905.

Un gran fisico.
Ritratto eseguito
da Reinhold Thiele
per Mr. Murray,
l'orgoglioso
vincitore della
competizione di
body-building
di Sandow, 1905.

14. Children
Los más pequeños
Bambini

The street could be almost anywhere in the Western world. The clothes and the boots that the little girl is wearing are those of 1905. But the smile is universal and eternal.

Esta foto podría pertenecer a cualquiera de las calles de una ciudad occidental. La ropa y las botas que lleva esta niña son típicas de 1905, pero su sonrisa es universal y eterna.

Potrebbe essere una strada di una qualsiasi città del mondo occidentale. I vestiti e le calzature della bambina sono del 1905. Ma il suo sorriso è universale ed eterno.

14. Children
Los más pequeños
Bambini

Slowly but steadily, life was becoming more comfortable for the very young, though poverty or a cruel Nanny could still bring infant misery. Children ceased to be 'little adults' and gained lives of their own. There were charities and foundations to protect children, to cater for their needs, to rescue them from the worst of plights. Psychologists claimed it was possible to understand the minds of children. At the Sorbonne, Alfred Binet believed he had even found a way of measuring their intelligence.

But children still posed problems for society. Discipline was rigorously imposed by passing adults. Few days passed in any school without the swish of the cane in every classroom. Policeman had no hesitation in boxing the ears of window breakers, apple scrumpers or any other 'little devils'.

During those rare times when children escaped from the adult world, they collected birds' eggs, fished for tiddlers, dammed streams, fought each other, got lost, were by turn kind and cruel to animals, and failed to take care of their clothes. It is to be hoped that they had fun, for a chain of events was already in progress that would viciously cut short the adult lives of millions of them in the next decade.

Lenta pero progresivamente, la vida era cada vez más amable con los más pequeños, aunque la pobreza o una niñera cruel aún amenazaban con sumirlos en la miseria. Por fin dejaron de ser "pequeños adultos" y pasaron a considerarse lo que en verdad eran. Había casas de caridad y fundaciones que les protegían, cuidaban de sus necesidades y les sacaban de todo tipo de apuros. Los psicólogos comenzaron a estudiar la mente infantil, hasta entonces olvidada por la ciencia. Alfred Binet, profesor de la Sorbona, afirmó haber descubierto un método para medir su inteligencia.

Pero los niños y las niñas eran todavía un problema para la sociedad. La disciplina de tiempos anteriores aún se imponía rigurosamente, y en las escuelas se podía oír el silbido de los bastones que usaban los maestros casi a diario. La policía no vacilaba en tirar de las orejas a los que rompían cristales, robaban manzanas o cometían otras pequeñas travesuras.

Tras escapar del mundo de los adultos, niños y niñas se dedicaron a vivir la infancia como debe ser: robaban huevos de los nidos de las aves, buscaban a sus amigos para jugar y deambular por las calles, se peleaban, se perdían, acariciaban a los animales y luego les pegaban, o se ensuciaban la ropa alegremente. Un mundo de diversión que, por el rumbo que estaban tomando los acontecimientos, en la década siguiente se convertiría para muchos de ellos, ya adultos, en un infierno de guerra y destrucción.

Ad un ritmo lento ma costante, le condizioni di vita dei più piccoli miglioravano sempre più, anche se la povertà, o una bambinaia crudele, potevano ancora far soffrire un piccino. I "piccoli adulti" di un tempo potevano ormai permettersi di crescere con più calma. Nascevano le istituzioni di carità e le varie organizzazioni che proteggevano i bambini, cercavano di soddisfare i loro bisogni e di salvarli dalle situazioni più disperate. Gli psicologi assicuravano che era possibile analizzarli e comprenderli, mentre alla Sorbona, Alfred Binet affermava di aver trovato il metodo per misurare la loro intelligenza.

Ma i bambini rappresentavano ancora un problema per la società. La disciplina veniva ancora imposta con estremo rigore dall'adulto di turno. Nelle classi, risuonavano spesso i colpi delle bacchette e la polizia non esitava a dare un ceffone a chi rompeva una vetrina o rubava una mela, o a qualsiasi altro "discolo".

Nei brevi spazi di tempo in cui riuscivano ad evadere dal mondo degli adulti, i bimbi andavano in cerca di nidi, catturavano pesciolini, sbarravano un torrente, litigavano fra di loro, si perdevano, giocavano con gli animali, a volte con affetto e altre con crudeltà e trascuravano puntualmente il loro modo di vestire. C'è da sperare che si divertissero, perché aveva già preso il via una serie di avvenimenti che avrebbero dolorosamente stroncato la vita di milioni di loro nel decennio successivo.

Water gypsies. It may have been an exceptionally warm autumn day or the water may have looked especially inviting. Paul Martin's photograph shows a group of lads getting dressed after a swim in the Serpentine, Hyde Park, London, October 1900.

Sin guardar la ropa. Puede que fuera un día de otoño inusualmente cálido o que el agua estuviera especialmente apetecible. Esta foto de Paul Martin muestra un grupo de chicos vistiéndose después de tomar un baño en el Serpentine de Hyde Park, Londres, octubre de 1900.

Vagabondi d'acqua dolce. Forse era una giornata d'autunno eccezionalmente calda o l'acqua aveva un aspetto specialmente invitante. La fotografia di Paul Martin mostra un gruppo di ragazzi che si rivestono dopo una nuotata nelle acque del Serpentine, Hyde Park, Londra, ottobre 1900.

Water babies. Doting, and hopefully strong, parents, give their children a swimming lesson in the River Thames at Wallingford, September 1906. Upstream, the Thames was relatively free from pollution.

Bebés de agua dulce. Unos padres atentos, y esperemos que lo bastante fuertes, dan una clase de natación a sus hijos en el Támesis a su paso por Wallingford, en septiembre de 1906. Aguas arriba, el río estaba relativamente poco contaminado.

Bambini d'acqua dolce. Dei genitori affettuosi e, almeno si spera, dalle forti braccia danno una lezione di nuoto ai loro pargoli sulle rive del Tamigi presso Wallingford, settembre 1906. Nel tratto più a monte, le acque del Tamigi erano relativamente incontaminate.

The children's playground on the roof of the Ellis Island Immigration
Centre, New York, c. 1905. The sides of the wagon are inscribed with
the words 'Uncle Sam'. A new patriotism was already taking over.

El patio de juego para niños en el tejado del Centro de Inmigración de
Ellis Island, en Nueva York, hacia 1905. A los lados del carro se puede
leer "Tío Sam": un nuevo patriotismo se extendía por Estados Unidos.

La terrazza del Centro d'immigrazione ad Ellis Island, utilizzata come
terreno di gioco, New York, ca. 1905. Sul fianco del carretto si distinguono
le parole "Uncle Sam". Stava già nascendo un nuovo sentimento patriottico.

The massed ranks of the Esperance Society Morris Dance Group arrives at Cumberland Market, May Day 1909.

Un autobús repleto de pequeños bailarines del Morris Group de la Sociedad de la Esperanza llegan al mercado de Cumberland, 1 de mayo de 1909.

Il Morris Dance Group della Esperance Society giunge al mercato di Cumberland in formazione compatta, 1º maggio 1909.

Boy Scouts at a camp in 1908. It was the year that Robert Baden-Powell founded the Scout movement and published *Scouting for Boys*. Six years later most of these boys would probably undergo more rigorous training.

Un campamento de *boy scouts* en 1908, el año en que Robert Baden-Powell fundó este movimiento infantil y publicó su libro *Scouting for Boys*. Seis años después, la mayoría de ellos recibirían probablemente un entrenamiento mucho más riguroso.

Alcuni boy scout in azione nel 1908. Era l'anno in cui Robert Baden-Powell fondava il movimento dello scoutismo e pubblicava *Scouting for Boys*. Sei anni più tardi, molti di questi ragazzi avrebbero partecipato a delle esercitazioni molto più rigorose.

A choir of angels – it is to be hoped. Choristers selected to sing at the Coronation of King Edward VII pose for the camera outside the Chapel Royal, St James's, London, June 1902.

Un coro de ángeles (¡esperémoslo!). Niños del coro elegido para cantar durante la coronación del rey Eduardo VII posan ante la cámara en el exterior de capilla real, en St. James, Londres, junio de 1902.

Un coro di angeli, si spera. Le voci scelte per cantare alla cerimonia di incoronazione del re Edoardo VII posano davanti alla cappella reale, Saint James, Londra, giugno 1902.

The one that didn't get away. London children admire
the catch of the day – a small gudgeon, 1905. Lakes in the
London parks were open to young anglers a hundred years ago.

El botín. En Londres, unos niños contemplan la captura del
día, un pequeño gobio, 1905. Hace cien años, se podía pescar
en los estanques de los parques londinenses.

La pesca del giorno. Alcuni ragazzini londinesi ammirano un
piccolo ghiozzo di fiume che non è riuscito a sfuggirgli, 1905.
Un secolo fa, i laghetti dei parchi di Londra erano aperti ai
piccoli pescatori.

The one that couldn't get away. The annual scramble for a piece of the Lenten Pancake at Westminster School, 1905. Traditionally, the chef tossed the pancake over a bar in the School Hall, and then scholars fought for the bits.

¡A por él! La competición anual por conseguir un trozo del pastel de Cuaresma en Westminster School, 1905. Según la tradición, el chef lanzaba el pastel al vestíbulo de la escuela y los alumnos se lanzaban a conseguir un trozo.

La caccia del giorno. La zuffa per un pezzo di dolce quaresimale che, per tradizione, ogni anno il cuoco della scuola lancia in aria da una barra, nel salone della Westminster School, 1905.

Working lads. Three pit boys from Newcastle, in the north of
England, 1909. School attendance was compulsory only up to the age
of twelve. From then on, most boys and girls looked to earn a living.

Niños obreros. Tres pequeños mineros de Newcastle, en el norte
de Inglaterra, en 1909. La escuela solo era obligatoria hasta los
12 años. A partir de esa edad, la mayoría de niños y niñas tenían
que buscar trabajo.

Piccoli lavoratori. Tre minatori di Newcastle, nell'Inghilterra del
nord, 1909. La scuola era obbligatoria solo fino ai dodici anni. La
maggior parte dei ragazzini e delle ragazzine cercavano subito un
impiego per guadagnarsi da vivere.

Watching lasses. A largely female crowd gathers to watch a Punch and Judy Show, 1905. The children are smartly dressed. Either this was a special occasion or it was a prosperous neighbourhood.

Un público infantil. Una multitud básicamente femenina, en un espectáculo de las marionetas Punch y Judy, en 1905. Van muy bien vestidos, lo que indica que era una ocasión muy especial o pertenecían a un barrio rico.

Piccole spettatrici. Un pubblico per lo più femminile assiste ad uno spettacolo di marionette, 1905. L'eleganza delle bambine fa pensare che si trattasse di un'occasione particolare o che provenissero da un quartiere benestante.

In the footsteps
of Sitting Bull.
The Indian wars
were long over, and
only cameras were
aimed at this young
Sioux brave in 1907.

Tras los pasos de
Toro Sentado. Las
batallas contra
los indios habían
terminado hacía
tiempo, y este joven
sioux solo debía
temer el disparo
de las cámaras,
en 1907.

Sulle orme di Toro
Seduto. La guerra
contro gli indiani
era finita da un
pezzo e nel 1907
solo una macchina
fotografica poteva
essere puntata
contro questo
prode Sioux.

In the footsteps
of Little Lord
Fauntleroy.
Master Prixley
enjoys his comic,
28 July 1903.

Tras los pasos
de Little Lord
Fauntleroy. Una
niña leyendo un
cómic, 28 de
julio de 1903.

Sulle orme del
piccolo Lord
Fauntleroy. Il
signorino Prixley
assorto nella lettura
dei suoi fumetti,
28 luglio 1903.

A lesson in oral hygiene, 1908. The slogan on the blackboard reads 'Spare the brush and spoil the TEETH'. Few people maintained a full set of teeth into adulthood at this time and most had a fear of dentistry.

Una lección de higiene bucal, en 1908. En la pizarra se puede leer: "Compartir el cepillo es estropear los dientes". En esa época, pocos niños llegaban a adultos con todos sus dientes y muchos le tenían un miedo terrible al dentista.

Una lezione di igiene orale, 1908. Lo slogan sulla lavagna recita: "Risparmiando il tuo spazzolino sciupi i tuoi DENTI". All'epoca, erano in pochi a mantenere una dentatura completa fino all'età adulta e tutti avevano una gran paura dei dentisti.

Never too young to learn. A mother gives her daughter a drop of the hard stuff at the bar of a public house, 1900. Licensing laws were less stringent at this time. Pubs stayed open all day and children were admitted.

Nunca se es demasiado joven para aprender. Una madre da a probar a su hija una bebida para adultos en un bar, 1900. Las leyes sobre consumo de alcohol eran menos estrictas que hoy. Los bares estaban abiertos todo el día y se permitía la entrada a los menores de edad.

Non si è mai troppo piccoli per imparare. Una madre dà alla figlia un goccio di "roba forte" al bancone di un pub, 1900. In quel periodo, le leggi sugli alcolici erano meno severe. I pub rimanevano aperti tutto il giorno e potevano entrarci anche i bambini.

There was little to keep children at home after school or on Sundays. They roamed the streets, seeking excitement. With luck they might find an ice-cream stall (opposite) or a game at the Chelsea Bridge Road Fair (above).

Al terminar la escuela y los domingos, nada podía impedir que niños y niñas salieran a la calle a jugar y divertirse. Con un poco de suerte encontraban un puesto de helados (página anterior), o un juego de feria, como en la foto, en la calle del puente de Chelsea (arriba).

C'era poco da fare per tenere i bambini in casa dopo la scuola o di domenica. Vagabondavano per le strade in cerca di divertimento. Con un po' di fortuna, potevano imbattersi in un venditore di gelati (pagina a fianco) o in un gruppo di giocatori alla fiera sulla Chelsea Bridge Road (in alto).

A generation earlier, children born with a handicap (the word was used freely then) received little special training or education. Here, blind boys from the Royal Normal College, Upper Norwood, London, perform on the parallel bars, July 1907.

Una generación antes, los niños que nacían con alguna discapacidad (entonces se solía usar la palabra *handicap*) recibían una formación y una educación especiales. En la foto, jóvenes ciegos del Royal Normal College, en Upper Norwood, Londres, hacen ejercicios en las barras paralelas, julio de 1907.

Una generazione prima, i programmi educativi speciali per bambini handicappati (all'epoca questa parola era usata liberamente) erano quasi inesistenti. Qui, dei giovani non vedenti del Royal Normal College, Upper Norwood, Londra, si esibiscono alle parallele, luglio 1907.

A writing class at the Oral Deaf and Dumb Institute, Fitzroy Square, London, 8 May 1908. Provision was erratic, and there was generally less help available in country districts.

Una clase de redacción en un centro para sordomudos, en Fitzroy Square, Londres, el 8 de mayo de 1908. El sistema educativo funcionaba de una manera un tanto caótica, especialmente en las zonas rurales.

Una lezione di scrittura presso l'Istituto per sordi e muti, Fitzroy Square, Londra, 8 maggio 1908. I corsi erano discontinui e in generale nelle zone rurali era ancora più difficile frequentarli.

Oh, the joys of drill in the schoolyard, 1906. And the steely eye of the teacher could spot any slacker among the 200 or so on parade.

Ejercicios gimnásticos en el patio de la escuela, 1906. La inflexible mirada del profesor era capaz de descubrir a los que no seguían el ritmo entre los más de 200 alumnos que llenaban el patio.

Che bello fare ginnastica nel cortile della scuola! E lo sguardo inflessibile del maestro poteva pizzicare immediatamente uno scansafatiche in mezzo ai circa 200 ragazzi schierati, 1906.

15. All human life
Cosas de la vida
Fatti della vita

The English take to the *piste*. A beginner sets out on the lower
slopes of (a rather flat) Northamptonshire, December 1908.
Her Edwardian clothing did little to help her in her struggles.

Los ingleses toman las pistas. Una esquiadora principiante se desliza
por las suaves pendientes de Northamptonshire, diciembre de 1908.
La moda eduardiana no estaba hecha para eso.

Gli inglesi si lanciano in pista. Una principiante affronta un leggero
pendio (piuttosto piatto) del Northamptonshire, dicembre 1908. Pare
che gli indumenti tipici di quel periodo non la aiutino molto nella sua
battaglia.

15. All human life
Cosas de la vida
Fatti della vita

New hopes, dreams, inventions and ideas brought a clutch of innovative eccentricities to a new century. The seriously deranged gave themselves shocks, endangered their lungs, challenged buses and lorries to tug-of-war contests, and flew their fluttering biplanes as close to the ground as possible – or even closer. The truly mad killed themselves in any number of imaginative ways.

Intrepid adventurers trudged further south or north than anyone had previously ventured. Everything and everywhere in the 1900s was the 'greatest' – the tallest, longest, newest, fastest, highest, lowest and often stupidest. Science thrilled amateurs and professionals alike, and its seemingly magic qualities delighted many. The world shrank. Whereas it had taken weeks for Britain to learn of the Indian Mutiny 50 years earlier, news could now cross the globe in a matter of minutes. East met west in unlikely places on unlikely occasions. People laughed and cried, danced and sang, lifted their spirits, sank into depression (a relatively new concept), loved and loathed, shrugged off the past and hastened to what they believed was a bright new future. Another decade came and went.

Junto con las nuevas esperanzas, sueños, inventos e ideas del nuevo siglo aparecieron personajes verdaderamente excéntricos. Los más extravagantes se aplicaban descargas eléctricas, ponían en peligro sus pulmones, desafiaban a autobuses y camiones en competiciones de fuerza, o volaban a ras de suelo con sus biplanos. Los más locos se suicidaban de formas inimaginables.

Los aventureros viajaban más lejos que nunca hacia el norte o el sur. A principios del siglo XX, todo tenía que ser lo mejor: lo más alto, largo o nuevo, lo más rápido o lo más lento y, también a veces, lo más estúpido. La ciencia emocionaba a investigadores y público por igual, y sus aparentes poderes mágicos divertían a muchos. El mundo era cada vez más pequeño. Cincuenta años antes, la noticia de un motín en India habría tardado semanas en llegar a Gran Bretaña. Ahora, las noticias cruzaban el planeta en cuestión de minutos. Oriente y Occidente se encontraban en los lugares y momentos más insospechados. La gente reía y lloraba, bailaba y cantaba, se alegraba o se deprimía (un concepto relativamente nuevo), se amaba y se odiaba, y por encima de todo intentaba olvidar un pasado decadente y se lanzaba hacia lo que prometía ser un futuro extraordinario. Una década más en el curso de la vida humana.

Nuove speranze, sogni, invenzioni ed idee apportavano al nuovo secolo una serie di novità davvero eccentriche. Un gruppo di squilibrati si applicava scosse elettriche, si avvelenava i polmoni, sfidava autobus e camion a una sorta di gare di tiro alla fune e volava con dei vibranti biplani fino a pochi centimetri da terra, a volte anche meno. Alcuni, pazzi del tutto, si inventavano dei suicidi davvero originali.

Avventurieri intrepidi rompevano le frontiere del sud e del nord, esplorando luoghi in cui nessuno aveva mai osato inoltrarsi. Nel primo decennio del secolo, tutto era "di più": il più grande, il più lungo, il più nuovo, il più veloce, il più alto, il più basso e spesso il più stupido del pianeta. La scienza faceva fremere allo stesso modo i dilettanti e i professionisti, mentre tutti rimanevano affascinati dalle sue qualità apparentemente magiche. Il mondo diventava più piccolo. Cinquanta anni prima, la notizia dell'ammutinamento dei sepoy aveva tardato intere settimane per arrivare in Inghilterra dall'India; ora le notizie facevano il giro del mondo in pochi minuti. L'Oriente e l'Occidente si incontravano in luoghi ed occasioni davvero inverosimili. La gente rideva e piangeva, ballava e cantava, era di buon umore o affondava nella depressione (una parola relativamente nuova), amava ed odiava, si scrollava di dosso il passato e accoglieva a braccia aperte ciò che per loro era un futuro nuovo di zecca. Un altro decennio era trascorso in un batter d'occhio.

Mysterious goings-on at a seance in Paris, c. 1900. Despite rapid developments in technology, education and communication, the 1900s witnessed a revival of interest in all things occult.

Fenómenos extraños en una sesión de espiritismo en París, hacia 1900. A pesar de los rápidos avances en tecnología, educación y comunicación, a principios del siglo XX renació el interés por las ciencias ocultas.

Fenomeni misteriosi durante una seduta spiritica a Parigi, ca. 1900. Malgrado il rapido sviluppo della tecnologia, dell'educazione e delle comunicazioni, questi anni furono testimoni di un rinnovato interesse per le scienze occulte.

Don't try this at home. Almost anything bizarre found its way onto a theatrical stage. Here, two men engage in a tug of war with a third who has the end of the chain fastened to a hook through his lip. Sadly, we do not know what they did for an encore.

Mejor no intentarlo en casa. Cualquier cosa que pudiera considerarse extraña tenía asegurado un lugar en el escenario. En la foto, dos hombres tiran de una cadena enganchada a los labios de un tercer hombre. No podemos imaginar qué hacían si el público les pedía un bis.

Non provate a farlo in casa. Qualsiasi stranezza trovava posto sui palcoscenici. Nella fotografia, due uomini praticano il tiro alla fune. All'altra estremità, l'avversario tira da un gancio conficcato in un labbro. Peccato che non sappiamo cosa abbiano fatto per il bis.

The wonders of civilisation. A German scientist poses by an Inca wall in
Cuzco, Peru, c. 1900. The stones of the wall have been numbered so that
it can be dismantled, carted off and rebuilt elsewhere.

Las maravillas de la civilización. Un científico alemán posa junto a una muralla
inca en Cuzco, Perú, hacia 1900. Las piedras han sido numeradas para poder
desmontarlas, trasladarlas a otro lugar y reconstruir la muralla.

Le meraviglie della civilizzazione. Uno scienziato tedesco in posa davanti a un
muro inca a Cuzco, Perù, ca. 1900. I blocchi di pietra sono stati numerati per
smontare la struttura, portarla via e rimontarla altrove.

The wonders of nature. Early 20th-century mountaineers cross a crevasse in the Alps, 1900. There were few places left in the world that bold amateurs were not prepared to explore.

Las maravillas de la naturaleza. Alpinistas de principios del siglo XX cruzan un barranco de hielo en los Alpes, 1900. Quedaban pocos lugares en el mundo que cualquier aventurero no se atreviera a explorar.

Le meraviglie della natura. Primi alpinisti del nuovo secolo attraversano un crepaccio sulle Alpi, 1900. C'erano pochi posti sul pianeta che gli intrepidi appassionati non fossero disposti ad esplorare.

Short rest. Swans are removed from a stretch of the River Thames near Henley to make way for the annual regatta, 1 June 1900. They appear to be used to the procedure.

Un breve retiro. Cisnes de un tramo del río Támesis, cerca de Henley, abandonan su hogar con motivo de la regata anual, 1 de junio de 1900. Parece que estaban acostumbrados a hacerlo.

Un po' di riposo. Alcuni cigni vengono evacuati dalla zona del Tamigi presso Henley per fare spazio alla regata annuale, 1° giugno 1900. Pare che per loro il trasferimento non rappresenti una novità.

Eternal rest. A flower-bedecked coffin reaches its final mooring after a journey by punt, 3 June 1903. Although it seems sadly romantic today, it may well have been the most practical way of getting the deceased from home to graveyard.

El reposo eterno. Un ataúd cubierto de flores llega a su destino tras un viaje en barca, 3 de junio de 1903. Aunque hoy pueda parecernos romántico, es probable que fuera la manera más práctica de conducir al difunto al cementerio.

L'eterno riposo. Una bara ricoperta di fiori al suo attracco finale dopo un viaggio in barca, 3 giugno 1903. Oggi potrebbe sembrare una scena romantica e malinconica, ma probabilmente era il modo più pratico per trasportare il defunto da casa sua fino al cimitero.

Muhammadan friars. Despite increasing persecution, the whirling dervishes continued to practise their religious ceremonies in 1905. The dance from which they took their name involved spinning round for 30 minutes, to achieve a trance-like state.

Frailes musulmanes. A pesar de sufrir persecuciones cada vez más duras, los derviches giróvagos seguían practicando sus ceremonias religiosas, 1905. La danza de la que toman su nombre consistía en girar durante una media hora para alcanzar un estado de trance.

Monaci musulmani. Nonostante le sempre più frequenti persecuzioni, i Dervisci continuavano a praticare le loro danze religiose nel 1905. Il ballo da cui prende il nome il loro movimento religioso consiste nel girare su se stessi per più di trenta minuti, con il proposito di raggiungere uno stato di trance.

Carmelite nun. This photograph of a sister praying in her cell was taken by Boyer d'Agen in 1904. The Order forbade its members turning to face a camera, or indeed anyone from the outside world.

Un monja carmelita. Esta foto de una monja rezando en su celda fue tomada por Boyer d'Agen en 1904. La orden de las carmelitas no permitía mostrar la cara a la cámara ni a nadie del mundo exterior.

Suora carmelitana. Questa fotografia di una religiosa in preghiera nella sua cella fu scattata da Boyer d'Agen nel 1904. L'ordine proibiva ai suoi membri di mostrarsi alla macchina fotografica, ma anche al resto del mondo al di fuori del convento.

Buildings crumble, fires break out and rubberneckers gather to stare in the aftermath of the San Francisco earthquake of 1906.

Edificios que se desmoronan, enormes incendios y curiosos que contemplan las consecuencias del terremoto de San Francisco, en 1906.

Edifici distrutti e incendi dappertutto. Una folla di curiosi contempla la tragedia dopo il terremoto di San Francisco del 1906.

As these two policemen attempt to escort an elderly lady across a London street, it would seem that one of the trio is having difficulty hearing what is being said. Even money says it's the sergeant on the right.

Dos policías ayudan a una anciana a cruzar una calle de Londres. Uno de ellos parece no oír demasiado bien, seguramente, el sargento de la derecha.

Due poliziotti cercano di aiutare un'anziana signora nelle strade di Londra. Pare che uno dei tre personaggi abbia dei problemi di udito, e non si tratta della dama.

In all their Victorian finery a group of ladies have a nice cuppa during an outing at Loughton, Essex, August 1908. No doubt high on the conversational agenda was the appalling decline in morals among the young.

Un grupo de damas con sus elegantes conjuntos victorianos toman el té religiosamente durante una salida a Loughton, Essex, en agosto de 1908. Es fácil adivinar que su tema de conversación era la degeneración de la moral entre la juventud de la época.

Un gruppo di donne in eleganti abiti vittoriani prendono una bella tazza di tè durante una gita a Loughton, Essex, agosto 1908. Senza dubbio il loro tema di conversazione favorito era l'inammissibile rilassamento dei costumi morali tra i giovani.

After a hard day ruling a subcontinent of some 300 million people, all a chap could do at the end of it was flop into a wicker chair, read the newly-arrived six-week-old copy of *The Times* and have a pedicure, Indian-style.

Tras una dura jornada gobernando un subcontinente de casi 300 millones de habitantes, no había nada mejor que hacer que sentarse en una cómoda butaca de mimbre, leer el *Times* que acababa de llegar, aunque fuera el de hacía un mes, y disfrutar de una sesión de pedicura al estilo indio.

Dopo una dura giornata passata a governare un subcontinente di circa 300 milioni di persone, il poveruomo non poteva far altro che sprofondare in una sedia di vimini, leggere una copia del *Times* di sei settimane prima, appena arrivato, e farsi il pedicure allo stile indiano.

Indian military representatives take tea on the terrace of the Houses of Parliament with the Unionist Chief Whip, Lord Valentia (centre), 1902. They were in England for the Coronation of Edward VII.

Militares indios toman el té en la terraza del Parlamento británico con el líder del Partido Unionista, lord Valentia (en el centro), 1902. Estaban en Inglaterra con motivo de la coronación de Eduardo VII.

Dei rappresentanti dell'esercito indiano prendono il tè sulla terrazza del Parlamento britannico in compagnia di Lord Valentia (al centro), capo del Partito unionista, 1902. Sono accorsi in Inghilterra per assistere all'incoronazione di Edoardo VII.

High-handed…
The impresario
Visser exhibits the
'celebrated dwarf'
named Beaufort
before the camera,
c. 1900.

Un peso ligero…
El empresario Visser
sostiene ante la
cámara al célebre
enano Beaufort,
hacia 1900.

Mano ferma…
L'impresario Visser
esibisce il "celebre
nano" Beaufort
davanti alla
macchina
fotografica,
ca. 1900.

Long-legged…
Possibly the tallest
woman in Britain
arrives in London,
26 May 1907.
She was booked
to appear at the
Hippodrome.

Piernaslargas…
La mujer más alta de
Gran Bretaña llega
a Londres, el 26 de
mayo de 1907, para
actuar en el
Hipódromo.

Gambalunga…
Una donna,
quasi sicuramente
la più alta della
Gran Bretagna,
arriva a Londra, il
26 maggio del 1907,
per un'esibizione
all'Hippodrome.

It required a mixture of ingenuity, patience and exploitation on the part of trainers to produce a team of football-playing dogs in June 1908. Whether the public was impressed is not known, but the scene has a 'backyard' look to it.

Se necesitaba una buena dosis de ingenuidad, paciencia y mano dura por parte de los entrenadores para formar un equipo de fútbol perruno, junio de 1908. No sabemos si el público aplaudía las jugadas, pero al menos tenían portería.

Ci voleva un misto di ingenuità, pazienza e di tirannia da parte degli allenatori per mettere insieme una squadra di calcio canina, giugno 1908. Magari il pubblico ne rimaneva molto colpito, comunque sia la scena ha un aspetto piuttosto "casereccio".

Less enjoyable, from the animal's point of view, was the life of this dancing bear in London, c. 1900. The poor creature spent its nights in confinement and its days padding the city streets, earning its owner a living.

La vida de este oso bailarín, en Londres, hacia 1900, era probablemente mucho menos divertida, como mínimo desde su punto de vista. El pobre animal se pasaba las noches encerrado y los días recorriendo las calles de la ciudad para dar sustento a su amo.

La vita di questo orso ballerino a Londra pare sicuramente assai meno divertente, ca. 1900. Il povero animale passava le notti in gabbia e di giorno doveva scarpinare per le strade della città per far guadagnare qualcosa al suo proprietario.

Paris, 1900. Framed by the girders of the 12-year-old Eiffel Tower is the
Trocadero, centre-piece of the Paris Exhibition on the Quai d'Orsay.
It was Europe's biggest fair, covering 547 acres (220 hectares).

París, 1900. Al fondo, enmarcado por las vigas de la Torre Eiffel, levantada
hacía 12 años, se ve el Trocadero, el edificio principal de la Exposición de
París, junto al Quai d'Orsay. Fue la feria más grande de Europa, con una
extensión de 220 hectáreas.

Parigi, 1900. Incorniciato dalle travi della torre Eiffel, ormai dodicenne,
il Trocadero era l'edificio principale dell'Esposizione di Parigi sul Quai
d'Orsay. Era la fiera più grande d'Europa, con i suoi 220 ettari di superficie.

London, 1908. Reinhold Thiele's reflective study of the Indian-style Court of Honour at the Anglo-French Exhibition at the White City. Later the same year, a part of the site was the setting for the Olympic Games.

Londres, 1908. Estudio de Reinhold Thiele sobre los reflejos de la Court of Honour, de estilo indio, en la «Exposición anglofrancesa» celebrada en White City, que unos meses más tarde sería el escenario de los Juegos Olímpicos.

Londra, 1908. Reinhold Thiele analizza il gioco di riflessi della Corte d'onore dell'Esposizione anglo-francese a White City. Nello stesso anno, una parte del recinto ospiterà i Giochi Olimpici.

The old, the frail and possibly the lazy travel to the Paris International Exhibition of 1900 by Bath-Chair. For the porters it was perhaps as well that the Exhibition was held in the city centre.

Los viejos, los enfermos y, seguramente, los holgazanes se dirigen en carritos a la Exposición Internacional de París en 1900. Para los que les llevan, es una suerte que la Exposición se celebre en el centro de la ciudad.

L'età, la fragilità o semplicemente la pigrizia conducono i personaggi della fotografia all'Esposizione internazionale di Parigi del 1900, su una sedia a rotelle. Probabilmente per i portantini era una fortuna che l'evento avesse luogo nel centro della città.

A view down Eyre Street Hill in the City of London, 1907. At the time it was London's version of Little Italy, the home of the Italian community. Today it is fashionable Clerkenwell, though still a very Italian part of London.

Una perspectiva desde lo alto de Eyre Street, en la City de Londres, en 1907. Esa zona era como el Little Italy neoyorquino, el corazón de la comunidad italiana. Hoy se llama Clerkenwell y es un barrio de moda, todavía con aires italianos.

Una veduta di Eyre Street Hill nella City londinese, 1907. All'epoca, il quartiere costituiva la versione inglese del Little Italy, area abitata da immigrati italiani. Oggi la zona prende il nome di Clerkenwell ed è una parte di Londra che conserva ancora un forte accento italiano.

The scene is a
Midlands street.
The theme is
eternal. The
costumes are
those of 1904.
Boy and girl step
out on a Bank
Holiday morning.

El escenario es una
calle cualquiera. El
argumento es el más
antiguo del mundo.
Dos enamorados,
vestidos al estilo
de 1904, pasean
abrazados en una
soleada mañana
de domingo.

La scena si svolge
in una strada delle
Midlands inglesi nel
1904. Gli abiti sono
tipici del periodo.
Un tema senza
tempo: un ragazzo
sottobraccio ad una
ragazza approfittano
del mattino di un
giorno festivo per
fare una passeggiata.

Index

Althorp, Lord 253

Barraclough, Sydney 256
Barnum, Phineas T 217
Barrie, J M 241
Beaufort 388
Binet Alfred 348–349
Blériot, Louis 7, 9, 11, 294–295
Bolm, Adolphe 221
Braque 222
Brennan, Louis 308
Brooke, Colonel Douglas 266
Bunsen 270–271

Campbell, Henry H 79
Carnegie, Andrew 34
Carr, Robert 324–325
Caruso, Enrico 222–223, 230
Chevalier, Maurice 212
Chekhov 222–223
Churchill, Winston Spencer 28
Clifford, Camille 246, 257
Cody, William Frederick ('Buffalo Bill') 214
Coffey, J K 217
Colver, Bert 310
Conan Doyle, Sir Arthur 335
Cook, Thomas 166–167
Corbett, Jim 318–319
Cortot 222–223
Curie, Marie 270–271, 283
Curie, Pierre 270–271
Cust, Sir Charles 300

Dare, Phyllis 210, 267

Dare, Zena 210
De Falla 222–223
Debussy, Claude 235
Degas, Edgar 243
Deslys, Gaby 250
Diaghilev 222–223
Duncan, Isadora 238–39
Durkheim Émile 66–67

Edward VII, King 16, 18
Einstein, Albert 270–271, 282
Elgar 222–223
Ewry, Pat 320

Farman, Henry 312–313
Fitzsimmons, Bob 336
Ford, Henry 301
Forster, E M 222–223
Freud, Sigmund 66–67, 222–223

Galli-Curci 222–223
Gandhi, Mohandas 30
Gibson, Charles Dana 7, 9, 11, 246
Goldsmith 317
Gorky, Maxim 233
Grace, Frederick 344
Grace, William Gilbert Dr 331

Hari, Mata (Margarete Geertruida Zelle) 198–199
Hayes, John 334
Hewitt 317
Higgins, Louis 57
Hoey, Iris 268
Houdini, Harry (Ehrich Weiss) 202

Jaurès, Jean 32
Jeffries, James J 318–319, 337
Johnson, Jack 318–319
Jo Jo 217

Karsavina, Tamara 226
Kruger, Paul 19

Laloo 217
Lang, Mathieson 194
Lenin, Vladimir Ilyich 25
Leno, Dan 207
Llangattock, Lord 300
Lloyd George, David 31

MacDonald, Ramsay 33
Mahler, Gustav 222–223, 234
Mann, Thomas 222–223
Marconi, Guglielmo 272
Martino, Signor 203
Matuchenko 54
McKinley, William 26–27
Melba, Nellie 222–223, 231
Méliès, Georges 196–197, 218–219
Mistinguett (Jeanne Marie Bourgeois) 213
Mithelstadt, Jakob 97
Mordkin, Mikhail 227
Morgan, John Pierpoint 35
Morris, James 217
Murray, Mr 345
Muybridge, Eadweard 238

Neaver, Carl and Mark 262

Nicholas II, Tsar 20–21
Nijinsky 222–223

Oakley, Annie 215
Oliver, Joe ('King') 222–223

Paderewski 222–223
Pankhurst, Christabel 60
Pankhurst, Emmeline 60
Pavlova, Anna 222–223, 227
Pethick-Lawrence, Lady Emmeline 59
Picasso 222–223
Pickford, Mary 61
Pietri, Dorando 335
Plank, Max 270–271
Prixley, Master 361
Puccini 222–223

Rachmaninov 222–223
Ravel, Maurice 222–223
Renoir, Pierre-Auguste 237
Rodin, Auguste 222–223, 242
Rolls, Hon C S 300
Röntgen, Wilhelm Conrad 285
Roosevelt, Theodore 29
Rothschild family 168

Schönberg 222–223
Shaw, George Bernard 222–223, 244
Show As He Goes 75
Shrubb, Alfred 321
Spencer, 6th Earl 253
Stanislavsky 222–223
Stephen, Sir Leslie 245
Stephens, Stephanie 240

Stiles, Leslie 257
Stott, Miss Kennedy 261
Strindberg 222–223

Taylor, John 322
Thiele, Reinhold 19, 43–44, 280–281, 337, 345, 393
Tolstoy, Leo Nikolayevich 232

Tolstoy, Sonya 232
Toulouse-Lautrec, Henri de 236
Trott, Alfred 330
Trotter, Master 263
Twain, Mark 228

Valentia, Lord 387
Victoria, Queen 12
Visser (impresario) 388

Walker, Robert 324–325
Wells, H G, 222–223
Wilhelm II, Kaiser 20, 276
Woolf, Virginia (Virginia Stephen) 245
Wright, Orville and Wilbur 7, 9, 11, 296–297

Yeats, W B 229

York, Duke of (later George V) 300
Young Herman 217
Ysaÿe 222–223

Zola, Émile 222–223

gettyimages

Over 70 million images and 30,000 hours of film footage are held by the various collections owned by Getty Images. These cover a vast number of subjects from the earliest photojournalism to current press photography, sports, social history and geography. Getty Images' conceptual imagery is renowned amongst creative end users.

www.gettyimages.com

Más de 70 millones de imágenes y 30.000 horas de secuencias filmadas forman parte de las muchas colecciones que pertenecen a Getty Images. Éstas cubren un vasto número de temas desde los principios del periodismo fotográfico hasta la actual fotografía de prensa, deportes, historia social y geografía. Las imágenes conceptuales de Getty Images tienen renombre entre sus creativos consumidores.

www.gettyimages.com

Le varie collezioni di proprietà della Getty Images comprendono oltre 70 milioni di immagini e 30.000 ore di filmati che abbracciano un ampio numero di soggetti: il giornalismo fotografico dalle origini ai giorni nostri, lo sport, la storia sociale e la geografia. Le immagini concettuali della Getty images sono rinomate fra gli utenti finali del settore creativo.

www.gettyimages.com